Praise for *Denver to Mumbai*

This book is an emotional account of Sawant's return to India after almost a decade living in America. With evocative language the author describes the Mumbai of her youth and the different reality she finds upon her return. Efficiency, the key word in the call centers that sprout all over the city, doesn't translate to other areas of everyday living, including broken promises in the delivery of custom furniture. This is a book that anyone who's ever lived outside of their native country or is fascinated by Indian culture will love. I highly recommend it.

—Lorenzo Pablo Martinez, author of the award-winning *Cuba, Adiós*

A great read for people around the world who have faced challenges of an international move. This is a heartwarming story of a woman juggling between her duties as a daughter and a mother, striving for her dream of a happily ever after. Hemangi's articulate account of her experiences in the USA and India is replete with humor and wit and is relatable to parents as well as immigrants. Best wishes to Hemangi in her new endeavor.

—Kadambini Dharap, Poetess of *Kinara Houn Apanach*

Sawant paints her family's aspirations, struggles, successes, joys, compromises, disappointments, and once-in-a-lifetime experiences in so much detail and clarity that I truly felt like I was sitting alongside her, listening to her tell her story.

—Mozelle Jordan, Professional Editor

I was so immersed in reading and could visualize the scenes so clearly and could relate to so many events that I've experienced in Mumbai. I must say it's a brilliant piece of work done by the author.

—Advocate Vivek Anand

DENVER
TO
MUMBAI

DENVER
TO
MUMBAI

A Story of Returning Home

HEMANGI SAWANT

SAGE PUBLISHING HOUSE

Paperback ISBN: 979-8-9916072-0-9
Hardcover ISBN: 979-8-9916072-2-3
eBook ISBN: 979-8-9916072-1-6

Published by Sage Publishing House

Sagepublishingemail@gmail.com

Book Design by Asya Blue Design
Cover Design by authorsupport.com

Disclaimer: This is a work of creative nonfiction. All the events in this memoir are true to the best of my memory. I have tried to re-create events, locales, and conversations from my memories of them. To protect privacy, in some instances, I have changed the names of individuals and places; I may have changed some identifying characteristics and details such as physical properties, occupations, and places of residence. Although I have attempted to ensure that the information in this book was correct at press time, I do not assume and hereby disclaim any liability to any party for any loss, damage, or disruption caused by errors or omissions, whether such errors or omissions result from negligence, accident or any other cause. The author in no way represents any corporation or brand mentioned herein.

BONUS OFFER

As a reader of my book, I have a **free gift** for you:
Top 10 Tips to Connect Kids to The Homeland Culture.

www.hemangi.com

To My Baba
because he ignited the light.

CONTENTS

INTRODUCTION

The Call That Changed My Life

It felt like just another ordinary afternoon on that warm day in May 2002. I played with my three-and-a-half-year-old son, Ronak, at our home outside of Denver. Suddenly, around two-thirty p.m., I was struck with an urge to sing an old *bhajan*. While Ronak continued to play with his toys, I got out my harmonium, a type of pump organ, and began singing as my fingers danced across the keys. As I sang this Indian devotional song, my heart and soul soared with feelings of gratitude while my eyes filled with tears.

Later, I encouraged Ronak to take his afternoon nap, but driven by a post-lunch surge of toddler energy, he refused. So, I let him play with his toy animals while I turned my attention to the book I'd been reading.

My landline rang, startling me. *Must have dozed off*, I thought. I picked up the phone and heard the voice of my younger sister, Shyamal, calling from India. I glanced at the clock; it was five p.m. in Denver, which made it four-thirty a.m. in India. "Hi. Why are you calling so late?"

"Is Ronak around?" She sounded tense, nervous.

Ronak appeared in the doorway, as he'd heard me answer the phone.

"Don't say it out loud, for Ronak's sake," she warned.

My initial confusion gave way to fear. "Say what?" I asked.

Shyamal took a deep breath before answering. "It's Dad. He's no longer with us. He passed away around two this morning, after a heart attack."

My stomach lurched. I couldn't speak as I began to sob uncontrollably.

Sitting down beside me, Ronak innocently looked at my face and asked, "Mommy, what's wrong?"

On the other end of the line, my sister pressed, "Control yourself, Sis. Don't cry so much. Ronak will be worried and confused."

I was heartbroken but grateful for her advice. Wiping my tears and clearing my throat, I gave Ronak a quick side-hug. "Don't worry, *beta*," I reassured him, stroking his dark, wavy hair. "Mommy's okay. You go play in your room while I talk to Maushi."

Realizing something as Shyamal shared more details, I said, "No wonder I felt an invisible push to sing *bhajan* just about the time when Dad's pain began." As she continued describing Dad's demise, my biggest concern was my mom and sisters.

"I'll be on the first flight I can book," I said.

When my husband, Neeraj, came home from work that evening, he was as shocked as I was about Dad's death. Neeraj arranged the next day's travel for Ronak and me on a Lufthansa flight from Denver. As a mourning daughter, I could have left my son at home and taken any uncomfortable flight alone from the East Coast, where there are multiple daily departures for India, but as a mother,

I had to ensure there were tickets available not just for me but for Ronak as well.

With our travel plans secured, I phoned Mom in India. *What do I say to a person who's just lost her spouse of thirty-five years?* I pondered. "I'm so sad this happened, Mom," I told her. "How are you? I'll be there soon. I'm leaving on a five thirty p.m. flight."

Mom replied in a heavy voice, "Do come if you can, but make sure Ronak is okay. You know your dad never liked making anyone wait, and everyone is already gathering, so I'm going ahead with the rites and rituals, rather than wait for you."

I was crushed but told myself, *Mom knows what's best.* "I should be there in twenty-four hours, as the flight takes that much time. So, can you wait?" I tried to persuade her again, but she was determined. I didn't say much, but I admired her strength in dealing with unimaginable pain.

Once Ronak and I were on the plane to India, I couldn't stop thinking about my father. I had recently been phoning day and night to check on him, and one particular call from just the previous week stood out in my memory. Dad had said, "I feel like seeing Ronak and you again."

"I know, Dad, but we were just there visiting you three months ago and will visit again in a few months," I said, not knowing the extent of his illness. At the same time, I was thinking to myself, as I had so often, *If we moved back to India, I'd be closer to my parents, and Ronak would have a chance to see all four of his grandparents regularly and get to know them so much better.*

It was three months before Dad's passing when I first learned of his illness and decided to visit him, back in February 2002. During that trip, Dad and Ronak connected so well, so naturally, that it felt as if Ronak, with his round face, big brown eyes, and beautiful, innocent smile helped Dad forget about his ailments while bringing him moments of happiness and joy. Now, in May 2002, after twenty-four hours of travel from Denver, we disembarked at the Mumbai Airport, and my sympathetic cousin, Rajesh, was there to pick us up. When we reached Mom's house, everyone was there; my mom, sisters, uncles, aunts, and cousins; but, of course, my father was absent—forever.

I still couldn't accept that Dad was gone. Ronak remembered him from our last visit, but now, he could only see Dad in a photograph in the living room, with a garland draped around the frame and a lit *diya* (oil lamp) beside it, per Hindu custom. Ronak was too young to put his feelings into words, but he searched for my dad in every corner of the house. I was stunned with grief.

Looking at Ronak, my grandma said with her eyes welling up, "Ankush would have enjoyed more of his grandson's company. Ronak is processing his grief by searching for his grandfather."

Overwhelmed, I held Ronak on my lap while Mom sat next to us, and we tried to explain to him that Grandpa now lived with God, but he would be watching over us from God's house and sending us his blessings. I hoped that image brought my grieving son some comfort.

Dad's demise was especially shocking because he had retired only fifteen days earlier. His health had deteriorated rapidly over the next thirteen days, and he'd passed away on May 14th. He was not happy with his retirement, as he always believed in the principle that work is worship. Just two years earlier, after learning that the Indian government had pushed the mandatory retirement age from fifty-eight to sixty, Dad had been delighted to continue teaching and remained as a vice principal of Mithibai College for two more years. Dad was a handsome man with a thick mustache and hazel-brown eyes. He always dressed elegantly for any occasion, and as a skilled orator, he was ready with a speech for any event. An accomplished writer, he had plans to practice law with his law degree and keep writing after retirement. Given Dad's ambitions and well-defined goals, none of us had ever imagined that his journey would end at age sixty.

Because the cremation had taken place before we arrived, I couldn't even see Dad for one last time, and I found it extremely challenging to process my grief. Blinded by anguish, I would sometimes sob non-stop whenever I was alone and did not find closure for years to come.

As I watched little Ronak search the house for Grandpa, I so wished my son had had more time with his grandfather to gain his guidance and benefit from his wisdom. As a mother, I had always felt that my child should know his grandparents, meet our extended family, experience our culture, and most importantly, know his roots. Relocating to India, our homeland, had been on my mind and heart for quite some time, but this devastating loss deepened my resolve to move sooner.

With that seed firmly planted in my mind, I returned to Denver, Colorado three months after my dad's passing. Still, it would be another seven years before we put our plan to move to India into action.

So, why am I sharing my story now?

My biggest inspiration remains my dad. I have always admired my father's books, his writing, and his aura. Alongside his teaching career, Dad focused on his literary work. In addition to numerous academic textbooks, he had five books to his credit. When he was my professor in my sophomore year, he encouraged my writing. I always wished to follow in his footsteps and write someday, even though my career had so far taken a different path. I had earned a psychology degree, and leveraging my marketing management diploma and software credentials, I am presently managing the software company I founded with my husband.

I arrived in the United States from Mumbai in my twenties, and over the years, I often thought of writing about my life experiences in America—in many ways, a life served on a silver platter. However, those early years in the U.S. were so busy with my newly married status and my career, followed by the birth of my adorable baby boy, that my book took a back seat for a while. When Neeraj and I began to plan our move back to India in 2009, I searched high and low for a book to guide me through the process. Unable to find such a book, I decided it was finally time to write this memoir and share my own experiences in the hope of helping others.

After the smooth sailing of living in the U.S. for thirteen years, it felt like an adventure to move back to our country of origin. Although India had a robust and growing economy, it was still a developing nation, and we faced many challenges living alongside its 1.3 billion residents, especially settling in Mumbai, India's fast-paced economic capital.

We spent thirteen years in suburban America, followed by nine years of mastering and overcoming the challenges of India's swiftly growing metropolitan city. The stories I'll be sharing have been valuable lessons for me. It's my hope that they'll entertain and educate you, though they may puzzle you at times. And if you are a parent, I hope they'll prove heartening and perhaps, even inspiring.

Ultimately, despite some bumps in the road, our journey was successful, and much of what we learned can be applied to other situations. So, if you are a first-generation American citizen or an immigrant considering returning to your country of origin or anyone moving to another country, this book can help you:

- Anticipate the challenges the international move may pose for an entire family.

- Understand how we processed the changes we experienced.

- Learn how we prepared our child for the move.

- Recognize the difficulties an American child will face in a new country.

- Discover how we adjusted to the disparity between our expectations and reality.

- Understand a mother's and father's dilemma and their resolve to do what's best for their family.

This book has a unique structure. With the exception of the first chapter, "My Homebound Journey," the book's first two parts recount the events of our move in roughly chronological order. Beginning with part three, chapters treat various topics individually which may or may not fall entirely into a sequential order.

As a final note, I would like to point out that I am writing about these experiences from my own perspective and am using pseudonyms rather than real names to protect the privacy of the individuals involved.

I hope you gain as much from this book as I gained from the experiences that helped shape it.

☙

PART ONE

Comfortable But Unsettled

1

My Homebound Journey

We almost missed our international flight! It was eleven thirty p.m., May 28, 2009, and my mind churned as I waited with my ten-year-old son, Ronak, at Newark Airport for our overnight flight to India. We were in the terminal, but I felt as if I was standing at a crossroads: on one side, our comfortable, settled life in America, and on the other, an uncertain future in the land of my birth.

Our big, sturdy international luggage couldn't hold all our experiences in this country. In the thirteen years since Neeraj and I had married and lived in the U.S., we had collected so many beautiful memories that now raced through my mind—the fragrance of freshly mown grass in our backyard, the winter snowmen we'd built for Ronak, the friends we'd made, and Colorado's snow-covered mountain peaks, visible from vast portions of the state. Unfortunately, these experiences didn't make it into our bags. I already missed them, and I was still on American soil. *Will I ever see Denver again?* I wondered.

I'd joined Neeraj, a software professional at Oracle Corporation, in Denver, after our wedding in 1996. Before our wedding, we'd decided to stay in the United States for only two to five years and then return to India. But our plans changed after I also began working as a software consultant in 1998. Now, after thirteen years in the U.S., I was finally on my way back to India.

I remembered how nervous I was when I first came to the U.S., especially since it was my first time on an airplane and my first-ever experience traveling abroad. Now, after more than a decade in America and countless international flights, air travel no longer fazed me. No, this time, my anxiety was driven by more serious concerns.

Part of me was excited that we were finally making the move, but another part had questions. *Are we doing the right thing?* I asked myself, looking at my son's innocent and worried face. Never in my life had I seen an entire family uprooted like this. But then I remembered the courage I'd needed when I'd said goodbye to my home, my family, my friends, and my whole universe when I had left India to join my husband in the U.S. *At least, this time,* I reminded myself, *I'm returning to my motherland, rather than a mysterious and unknown place.* Still, that was a small comfort now, when my son's worried eyes gazed up at me and our journey half-way around the globe had begun with seemingly one hitch after another. The hassles and travel delays that we'd battled all day . . . were they a sign? A warning? All three of our flights that day had experienced hiccups. I realized that travelers always face the prospect of schedule changes and missed flights, but the thought that all our delays on this particular day might be an omen of harder times to come echoed loudly in my overanxious mind. To tell the truth, I felt apprehensive about the big move and, most importantly, how

Ronak would cope. Would he adjust well or be overwhelmed?

Neeraj, Ronak, and I had finished packing up our entire life in Denver just five days ago (although Neeraj would return to Denver to complete his project commitment), then had washed the dust off our hands, and flown across the country to don plastic mouse ears and wave at Mickey Mouse while eating ice cream at Disney World. This morning, we'd crammed our luggage into our rental car and drove to the Tampa Airport so Ronak and I could fly to Chicago, change planes, then proceed to Newark to catch our international flight to Mumbai.

It was almost noon when we reached the Tampa Airport. We didn't wilt in that scorching summer heat as we were still in our easygoing Disney-World-frame-of-mind. After spending four glorious days at the "happiest place on Earth," we had acclimated to the high temperatures of the Sunshine State.

Father-son duo at Cocoa Beach near Disney World,
Florida, a day before our departure to Mumbai.

Ronak was sad about the move, but the magic of Disney transformed his mood, and I felt he was slowly going with the flow, coming on board with our plans. As we stood inside the Tampa terminal, we quickly checked the flight information board and realized, to our horror, that Neeraj's flight to Denver and our Chicago flight would depart from opposite ends of the terminal. Like a skydiver without a parachute, my mind suddenly hit the ground, and we understood that Ronak and I had to say goodbye to Neeraj right then and there. From that moment on, it would be a long time before we'd be reunited as a family.

Neeraj struggled to put on a happy face for our son. "Happy journey, Ronak. Have fun in India, and I'll see you soon." Neeraj hugged Ronak and glanced away, trying to hide his misty eyes.

"And you have a safe journey to Denver," I told Neeraj with a heavy heart as I joined them in a family hug. We all felt blue thinking about being on two different continents for the next few months, but there was no other option—Ronak's Mumbai school was starting soon, and Neeraj had to return to his current project assignment in Denver.

By the time Ronak and I boarded our flight to Chicago, we already missed Neeraj. As our aircraft slowly taxied out to the runway, I noticed many planes lined up for takeoff. *This can't be good*, I thought. Our takeoff, scheduled for one p.m., still hadn't happened by one-thirty. When two p.m. rolled around and we were still on the tarmac, my patience started to wear thin. My fellow passengers looked around, skeptical and mumbling as the pilot instructed everyone to remain seated while we awaited our turn on the runway. I knew this delay would undoubtedly affect my connecting flights. I tried calling Air India from my seat, but to no avail. Luckily, I was able to reach Neeraj's cell phone and leave a voicemail asking him to contact Air India. As I hung up the phone, we began to taxi down the runway.

Miraculously, we made it to Chicago O'Hare in two hours. Not waiting for instructions from airline staffers at the door, I pushed through the crowd and ran with Ronak to the gate for our connecting flight to Newark, but alas! We were too late—our plane had already departed.

"Now what, Aai? Do we go back to Denver?" Ronak asked while I tried not to look distressed.

"No! We'll try to get on the next flight," I replied as we rushed to a nearby airline information desk. Fortunately, the staff found a flight to Newark leaving in thirty minutes and booked us seats. My relief was short-lived, however, when I realized that even after we reached Newark, we might still miss the Air India flight to Mumbai, especially considering the insufficient time for security check-in of our oversized luggage.

"Could you please inform Air India about our late arrival?" I urged the gate agent.

"I'm afraid we can't contact other international carriers," he said with a dismissive smirk.

So, in the next thirty minutes, Ronak and I apprehensively boarded our substitute flight to Newark. Rubbing my sweaty palms in that freezing cabin, I considered the logistical nightmare awaiting me in New Jersey. *How far apart are the domestic and international terminals at Newark? Will we have to take a shuttle bus or a train? Will there be room for all our luggage?*

During the previous thirteen years, I had traveled from Denver to Mumbai every summer, mainly on Lufthansa and twice on KLM.

I could have completed that journey blindfolded, as my bags were always checked from Denver directly to Mumbai. But this trip was different; flying Air India for the first time, I would have to collect our bags from the domestic baggage claim at Newark and recheck them with Air India for the flight to Mumbai. If we missed that flight, we would have to stay overnight, with all our luggage, and try to catch a flight the following morning.

Is missing the New Jersey flight a sign of things to come? I worried again, wondering what it might portend for our move. I tried to push all fears out of my mind, the biggest being that if Ronak did not adjust after a year in India, we would be compelled to return to Denver. Although Neeraj and I were confident in our job skill sets and ability to obtain suitable work opportunities in the U.S., we were not sure we could get our old jobs back. If we couldn't, Ronak would again have to adjust to a new home, school, new friends, and maybe even a new city in America. I dreaded putting so much weight on my young son's shoulders.

It was seven p.m. when we landed at Newark, only two and a half hours before our scheduled intercontinental flight departure. My forehead furrowed at the sight of the clock. At the baggage claim, I still had to find our four large bags from our earlier missed flight. Then, with Ronak running alongside the cart, we would have to catch the airport train to the international terminal.

We were waiting at the baggage claim when I felt a tap on my shoulder. "Hi, Hemangi! Load a few on my trolley."

I turned and saw it was my friend, Charu. She lived in New Jersey and had come to wish us bon voyage on our big adventure. I felt so happy and relieved to see her as we quickly divided the luggage between two carts. We scampered to the concourse, luggage carts in tow, searching for the airport train. A crowded sea of travelers awaited the train's arrival, and as soon as it did, everybody knew what to do except us. As people pushed past us, making us wait helplessly, we helped Ronak board the train first and tried to lug our overstuffed carts on board, but unfortunately, they got stuck in the door, amusing the less-burdened travelers.

"This never happens on the Denver Airport train," I muttered. Disappointed, we quickly pulled Ronak out and restlessly awaited the next train. It was now eight-thirty p.m., only one hour before our next flight. If Air India closed the check-in soon, we might also miss that flight. My heart thumped harder. With each passing minute, my stomach churned quicker, and my lingering doubts loomed large yet again. *Are these hurdles trying to tell me something?*

"Don't let anyone walk in before you push your cart in," I instructed Charu in our mother tongue, Marathi. Desperate times called for desperate actions. The carts required expert handling to avoid getting them stuck in the door, and maneuvering would be easier in an empty compartment.

"You help board Ronak first, then from inside the train, I'll help you pull your cart," Charu added.

On the next train, other travelers scoffed and rolled their eyes at our endeavors, but we were just glad to be on board with all our luggage intact.

Once disembarked, we desperately searched for the Air India ticketing desk; the information desk personnel said it was at the opposite corner of the floor. We rushed over, but on reaching that corner and unable to find it, I asked around, and someone said, "Air India? Never heard of it!"

With only thirty minutes remaining before takeoff, I was almost sure we'd miss the flight. But then my dad's wise words came to me: "To try and to search for the solution depends on you and rests solely in your hands." Following his advice, I pushed ahead. My throat was parched, but there was no time to waste, not even a minute to catch my breath. Fortunately, I saw an Indian couple strolling by and thought, *They must have come to see off their loved ones.* When I asked, they pointed out the ramp that led us to the lower level and directly to the Air India ticketing desk.

Finally, triumphantly, we had arrived! That joy, though, lasted only a few seconds when I realized it was now nine-twenty p.m.—only ten minutes before our scheduled departure. I scuttled to the counter and told the ticketing personnel my story in one frantic breath— the frustrating delay in Tampa, an unavoidably missed flight in Chicago, and how we almost hadn't made it to their ticketing desk.

"Your passports and tickets," the *saree*-clad ticket agent replied without looking up. I handed them over, then ran my fingers through my hair in an effort to look more put together. "Put the bags on the scale." She pointed to the scale, exhibiting a complete lack of sympathy.

But I overlooked her impolite manner, as it seemed like she might get us on the next flight. I wondered, *Are there many international flights from New Jersey to Mumbai?* In those days, Denver had only two flights a week to India, but New Jersey, being a busy East Coast airport, might well have more.

After printing our boarding passes, the agent said the flight had been delayed and would now take off at eleven-thirty p.m.

"Oh! Okay!" I sighed, this time at the familiarity of the delay. Even our final aircraft had arrived late and was undergoing cleaning and preparations for the long-haul flight.

"It's strange!" I said to Charu. "Today's highlights have included delays, a missed flight, and chaotic running through the airport; all three of our flights since morning have had hiccups." I vented my feelings. Relaxing in the departure lounge, we chatted for some time, but deep in my mind, I still worried, *Is this a sign? A glimpse into our big journey ahead: The Move? Or maybe my mind is playing tricks after facing so much stress and uncertainty in one day.*

Soon, Charu and I bid our goodbyes, and as Ronak and I moved with the crowd toward the security check-in, my thoughts still raced. Once onboard, Ronak immediately fell asleep. It was a fourteen-hour nonstop flight to Mumbai, and there would be plenty of time to check out the onboard entertainment selection later. So, I opted for a short nap before they began carting out meals.

Even while dreaming, my thoughts never slowed. As my mind raced over our decision to move, I kept coming back to that party at the Girkar residence about three months ago—that weekend almost seemed like it happened yesterday.

2

The Good Life in Colorado

Beautiful Colorado mountains.

The Soccer Game

As the dawn light peeked through the bedroom window and touched my face, I blinked and turned to the other side. It was six forty-five on a bright Saturday morning. Neeraj, being a light sleeper, opened his eyes and reminded me about Ronak's soccer game scheduled for that day.

"Let me wake Ronak up," Neeraj said and stepped out of our bedroom. "Already brushing your teeth, Ronak?" I overheard Neeraj say, perhaps seeing Ronak in the bathroom.

"No need to wake me up today, Baba!" Ronak exclaimed. I was impressed hearing this and began listening to the father-son conversation.

"Are you excited about your game?" Neeraj asked.

Ronak delivered his favorite line, "I was born ready!" and asked, "Baba, can you please get my backpack, shin guards, and cap out of the closet?"

"Sure. Here you go. Now, get ready and come down for breakfast," Neeraj said. Before heading downstairs to the kitchen, Neeraj returned to our room and asked, "Are you awake?"

"Good morning!" I yawned and scrambled out of bed on insufficient sleep. I had been up late watching the latest Bollywood movie the night before.

"Morning, get ready; I'm making tea," Neeraj said as he stepped out of the room.

I peered out the second-floor window into our backyard. The morning sunlight seemed to have draped everything in its warm blanket. As the light spread, it enhanced the green grass sprouting in patches. Fresh, young leaves and buds on trees were a delightful sight, heralding the arrival of spring. It was a gorgeous day to be outside. Ronak appeared in the yard and headed straight for the raspberry bushes, searching for some ripe berries for his breakfast. I watched him pluck the fruits and gather them in a mug, like an expert forager. He gazed at the raspberry bushes for a second and attempted to measure them against his just-over-four-feet height.

Those raspberry bushes were very dear to Ronak. He was five when we completed our backyard landscaping. Our landscaper insisted on planting at least five trees in the backyard to provide more privacy between our yard and the neighbors' houses. At the end of the project, he dug five holes for the trees of our choice, which he would help us plant later. Initially, I was not in favor of the idea of buying trees. I thought they would generate too many fallen leaves in the backyard that would need to be cleared, creating yet another weekend chore. Nonetheless, I reluctantly joined my family for a nursery visit. The variety of foliage in the nursery captivated us, and surprisingly, we all enjoyed learning the names of the trees.

Under the spell of those plants, we went overboard with six fruit trees and six flower bushes. Finally, to bridge the gap at the checkout counter between the actual cost and our budget, we settled on only two fruit trees, three bigger aspen trees, and two floral bushes. But we gave in to our child's wish to buy a raspberry plant he had selected. Neeraj immediately helped Ronak plant the raspberry bush in the backyard that afternoon, and Ronak completed the planting ceremony by watering it. Thereafter, every spring, when this bush bore fruit, Ronak would dutifully visit the backyard daily and handpick the berries. After washing them, he would share two or three raspberries with us and devour the rest. This day was no exception to his berry routine.

As I came down the stairs, I heard Neeraj calling Ronak for breakfast. A plate of warm chocolate chip waffles awaited him on the kitchen table.

"I got around ten to twelve berries today, but I can't wait to get eighty to ninety like last summer!" Ronak proudly announced as he entered the kitchen.

"Will Mom and Dad get a bigger share this summer?" I teased.

Soon, we finished our breakfast of waffles, eggs, berries, and our weekend special ginger-flavored chai and rushed to the car. Today's soccer game was an out-of-town match in Boulder, but we could be there in fifty-five minutes via the interstate.

As we drove, the front range of the Rockies escorted us along our left: beautiful, snow-covered mountains meeting the sunny blue sky. Yellow dandelions peeked through the greenery around us and swayed with the wind. This Colorado mountain scenery always reminded me of the song sequences in Yash Chopra's Bollywood movies, filmed mostly in Switzerland.

Eventually, enjoying the ever-changing spring landscapes, we reached Boulder. Those snow-peaked mountains caught Ronak's attention as we searched for the soccer field.

"Wow! There's still snow on the mountains. Should we go there?" He was probably daydreaming of snow tubing.

"Look!" I blurted, a little alarmed. "There are snow mounds all around the edges of the field. They probably had to shovel for the game." Now, I was worried about Ronak running over the snowy wet grass.

"Yes, Boulder got nearly eight inches of snow last week," Neeraj said as he parked our car near the field. I got out and opened the back door for Ronak.

"When it snows that much in our county, we get the day off." With this ingenious observation, Ronak stepped out of the car. He waved at his teammates standing at the other end of the soccer field and walked over, carrying his backpack.

"Are you excited for today's game, Ronak?" his assistant coach, Andy, asked while stepping out of his car, parked next to ours.

By now, almost fifteen feet ahead of us and glancing back, Ronak replied with a grin, "Yes, Coach!"

"Good morning, guys!" Andy greeted us.

"Morning, Coach! Have a great game today," I greeted him.

"And Let us know if we can help in any way," Neeraj added as we walked toward our team.

Some parents quickly surrounded Andy to discuss the upcoming game. In contrast, our players diligently prepared a few feet away—putting on shin guards, soccer shoes, and team jerseys. In the nick of time, Jared, the head coach, arrived and rescued Andy from the crush of parents. As Jared led the team's pregame warm-up exercises, most parents got comfortable in their camping chairs with their coffee or Gatorade, while others sat on outdoor blankets on each side of the field. But almost every parent was busy instructing their respective offspring with some last-minute advice.

"Hi, Hemangi. Can you give me a hand, please?" Savanna requested, walking behind my camping chair as she trudged toward the park benches with a heavy box. I swiftly helped her carry some snack bags from her Land Rover, while Neeraj helped her husband, Jim, move a big carton of Gatorade bottles.

"Tim's parents couldn't come today, so we got the snacks on their behalf," Savanna explained, sounding a little overwhelmed.

"Oh, are they okay?" I asked.

"Yes, fine. Tim's grandparents are visiting for the weekend. So, we've been rushing to the grocery store for the team snacks Heather and Andrew were supposed to bring."

"I'm so sorry; you should have called me!"

"They only informed me last night. As a team mom, I had to make arrangements and couldn't delegate it to anyone because it was a last-minute change," she said in one breath.

Once the game began, we eagerly took our seats. Seeing our offspring play these competitive soccer games was a wonderful feeling. As a defensive player, Ronak was relaxed in his position. One of his teammates, the very quick and steadfast Jack, was on the offensive line. He would expertly maneuver the ball, skillfully evading opposing players who tried to block him, and swiftly kick it in the opponent's goal. With Jack in charge, the other boys on the team could loosen up a bit.

Still, Jack and the other boys could never escape their parents' perpetual coaching from the sidelines. If the kids didn't follow those instructions, it seemed as if their enthusiastic parents might storm the field and kick the ball, scoring the goal themselves.

Some parents have an excessive regard for sports, I thought. Living in the U.S., we had learned that playing any sport is held in high esteem here. In contrast, at that time in India, if your child was not interested in cricket, then no other sport really mattered, and parents thought it best if their children focused on academics instead of sports. But Neeraj and I were just glad to engage Ronak in some sporting activity and keep him occupied in otherwise lonely suburban life in Denver.

Ronak's team won, and he and all his teammates were thrilled with their 10 - 5 victory. Soon, Savanna distributed bottles of Gatorade, packages of animal crackers, and cupcakes to our players. I liked this idea; that way, only one player's parents brought snacks for that particular day, and all the kids received identical snacks, keeping everyone happy. The postgame snack presented the opportunity for the kids to interact with one another. With less school homework and too much time on their hands, it was necessary that we engage the kids in activities so they didn't feel lonely and instead, developed a spirit of sportsmanship. Our helpful team coaches made that possible. Feeling grateful, we congratulated the coaches and thanked them for all their energy, enthusiasm, and efforts to train our kids throughout the season.

On our way home, Neeraj asked about our plans for the rest of the weekend.

"We have an invitation to a get-together at the Girkars' tonight," I said.

"I don't want to go to anyone's house today, Aai," Ronak muttered from the back seat.

"Then don't complain later that you're bored at home."

"No, I will do anything to not go to a Desi party." (We Indian Americans refer to each other as Desis.)

"Okay," Neeraj said, winking at me. "I'm making an executive decision—we won't go if you fold your own laundry." In the absence of any positive response from Ronak, Neeraj asked, "Do you want to see the new Disney movie tomorrow?"

"Yes, I want to see *Prince Caspian*[1]," Ronak replied swiftly this time, taking a break from sipping his Gatorade.

"Okay, we can catch the movie tomorrow, but we must go to the party tonight," Neeraj said.

Ronak nodded his agreement with this bargain.

During the week, our family danced to the clock's relentless tune, so occasionally, we tried to loosen up with a movie whenever PG-13 or Disney films played in local theaters. That way, we were guaranteed age-appropriate material for Ronak. In those days, only when Ronak had a sleepover or a playdate at a friend's house did Neeraj and I try to catch a non-Disney movie or any film rated above PG-13. The Narnia sequel, *Prince Caspian*, would be child-friendly viewing.

The Desi Party

Later that evening, we arrived at the dinner party. I was thrilled that I could wear a *saree*. This colorful drape always lifts my mood. Indeed, it was a pleasant change after wearing business casual to the workplace every day. I urged Ronak and Neeraj to dress up in Indian *kurtas* (long tunics) but convinced only Ronak.

At the Girkar residence, fifty pairs of footwear obscured the porch. Suman welcomed us with a broad smile and her deep-set dimples. I handed her the flowers and cake we'd brought. A lot of our friends were already there, primarily work colleagues—all Indian families: Mehra, Iyer, Verma, Tawade, and Chakraborty. I was happy to see the Vermas there since Pranav would be the perfect friend for Ronak at the party. Typically, in our circle, our kids knew each other well. As always, they were sent to the basement to play. The host family had a movie screen and table tennis in the basement, so the kids were happy to get away from their parents.

After the usual pleasantries, the women, dressed in our colorful *sarees*, assembled in the family room. Comfortably perched on the sofa and chairs around a coffee table, we helped ourselves to appetizers like *samosas*, spring rolls, and quiche from platters on the center table. The men moved to the sundeck where Ajay, our host, was busy making drinks for everyone. Ajay politely stopped by in the family room to ask what we'd like to drink. "Ladies, I am taking special requests for margaritas, mocktails, cocktails, or wine."

"Are you sure? Mocktails sound like a lot of work." We didn't want to overburden our host.

"Don't worry! I'll pass on the requests, and your spouses will work on executing your orders."

We all laughed and placed our orders.

Meanwhile, I helped Suman put a fresh batch of appetizers from the oven onto a tray and carried it to the deck where the men were busy making drinks. Subjects like the current job market and the OCI (Overseas Citizenship of India) card versus the PIO (Person of Indian Origin) card after citizenship topped the discussions on the deck. Because most of us present at the party had obtained our American citizenship around 2004, these topics always dominated the conversations.

Our drinks awaited us when Suman and I rejoined our friends in the family room.

"Oh, I miss India! Those days, we ate so much *chatpata* food." Lalita sounded nostalgic for the tangy foods of our homeland as she sipped a margarita and nibbled a *samosa*.

"The best part is eating yummy food on the beach!" Bimal Verma added.

"Gosh, I miss the beach the most," I said. My old Mumbai memories surfaced as I gazed at my margarita glass, perfectly decorated with a slice of pineapple over a salt-covered rim.

"They have a variety of sweets, and available daily too." Hailing from inland, Namita didn't fully share my longing for the beach, so she steered the conversation back to food.

"And you can get it all home-cooked fresh in India," Sarita added with a sigh. "There are cooks available for daily work."

"Not just cooks, they also have help for dusting, sweeping, dishwashing, and ironing," Neelima chimed in wistfully.

"Here, in the U.S., we work outside the home but cook and clean our homes too, while they have so much help out there," Veena agreed. "Gosh, I envy people in India."

"Near my in-laws' place in Gujarat," Anamika said, "this ice cream parlor sells ice cream made of *paan* (betel nut leaves). It was the best. It's been five years since we visited India, but I still remember the taste." She grew misty-eyed with her memories.

We all started imagining the *paan*-flavored ice cream with her. These Desi parties always put me in that nostalgic trance and strengthened my decision to move back to India.

Amid this fun soiree, my mind played its typical tennis match—I was moving to India with my family in the next three to four months. I'd never thought I would stay in America for more than two years, but after thirteen years, I was still here and missed India dearly.

As time passed, Neeraj and I had acquired our green cards before eventually gaining our American citizenship. By then, I had begun to feel comfortable in my American home. Nevertheless, we always planned to move back before Ronak reached a certain age, so he could acclimate with an open mind and be less resistant to the change.

There was no point announcing our move to everyone yet, as we still had to complete a few preparations to support our decision. We had found an apartment in Mumbai, but Ronak's school admission and enrollment, along with our job search, plane tickets, furniture shipments to India, selling off the remaining things, and much more on the list, still awaited resolution. If the school admission wasn't completed in time, we'd have to put off our departure date for a year. Knowing it was too soon to reveal our plans, I immersed myself in those precious, gleeful moments with my girlfriends at the party. After all, for the past thirteen years, those families had been our surrogate families away from our birth country.

Even with lovely weekends spent watching Ronak play soccer and evenings celebrating with friends, I still deliberated about our move back to India. Neeraj and I both were happy with our IT jobs, which offered us lots of flexibility to build our family schedule around office time. On weekdays, one of us would take Ronak to school by eight a.m. The other parent would pick him up at three-thirty, in time for Kumon (an after-school math and reading program) on Mondays and Wednesdays, and soccer if it was Tuesday or Thursday. Our family life was jam-packed with homework on weekdays, after-school recreation, and meal preparation. Sometimes, with our daily routine bursting with activities, we barely realized that we had made it to the weekend.

Sunday

The previous night's party left a tangle of memories in my mind; no one had questioned Lalita or complained when she had gone off on a tangent, glorifying Indian food and jewelry. In a way, she had helped everyone dig deep into their memory banks and re-experience those gastronomic wonders.

I woke up to another beautiful day—Sunday. Ronak was still in bed and pretty tired after the get-together. Dressed in my workout clothes, I grabbed my cap and slipped on my Nikes for my morning walk. Putting on my headset, I looked at the park from our porch to gauge the weather. Though it was a sunny morning, I noticed that only two parents with their kids were using the swing set, and they were wearing heavy coats. Still, it felt good to at least see somebody in that huge park. I put on my warm jacket, started my playlist of songs, and began my routine walk toward the park.

After twenty minutes, I saw a couple walking from the opposite direction. As they neared me, the woman wished me good morning; I smiled and greeted them. It's a Colorado custom that strangers smile and greet each other. And living here for so long, we had adopted those unstated norms. I liked the way strangers so often commented about the weather, and there was a more profound appreciation, especially for a day like this—chilly, but with a gorgeous, bright, clear sky and sunshine adding to the morning's pristine beauty.

After completing the walking track, I heard someone call my name. Dressed in black, my neighbor, Crystal, with her brown hair in a ponytail, walked over and hugged me.

"Long time, no see," I said.

"Can't wait for summer. I'm looking forward to the fruits in our backyard. I'll share a few." She smiled broadly.

"Sure, I would love that. We will also share raspberries from our backyard, if we can get Ronak to part with any."

We chatted until we reached my mailbox at the end of our driveway; I picked up the mail and bid goodbye to Crystal. I was glad to see the letter from a company that shipped containers internationally. If I found the information I needed in that envelope, it would bring us one step closer to our goal.

I entered the house with feelings of elation and a handful of mail. It was ten a.m., which raised the question, *What do I cook for breakfast?*

Ronak and Neeraj were playing badminton in the backyard, so I stopped to watch for a minute; I couldn't miss Ronak keeping his dad busy running after the shuttlecock. With Ronak out of the kitchen, I quickly got the *dosa* batter (made of rice and split black gram) from the refrigerator. In my relentless, motherly efforts to cook nutritious homemade food, I made *uttapam* (pancake), adding only a little orange food coloring and salt. I topped it with chopped tomatoes, bell peppers, mushrooms, and onions and flipped it in the pan to cook the side with the veggies. Unfortunately, Ronak had shown a dislike for rice products since his early years. The sugarcoated name and theatrical presentation as "Indian pizza" was the only way I could ever get the *uttapam* into his system.

We enjoyed *dosas*, chutney, and chai for breakfast while Neeraj and I read the container shipment information. Ronak nibbled at the Indian pizza with ketchup, his eyes fixed on the TV. Hours later, he was still laser-focused.

"Ronak, did you finish your Kumon homework?" He always detested this question, but I had to ask when I saw him sprawled in front of the TV later that afternoon.

Eyes still glued to the screen, he gave his standard answer. "Yes, I will, in five minutes."

Like other American Desi parents, we had enrolled Ronak in an after-school math and reading program at Kumon, a learning institute that helped students with mathematics and English proficiency. Kumon was very popular among Indian and other Asian parents, so 70 percent of Ronak's Kumon classmates were Asian. After full days at school, he attended Kumon twice a week, though he never seemed to enjoy it. If I had to complete extra homework, in addition to my regular school homework, I would be uninterested too. But being parents of Indian descent, Neeraj and I continually compared our child with his counterparts in the Indian educational system. Those children knew all their arithmetic tables up to twenty-five by fourth grade, had a vast English vocabulary, and always passed their classes with flying colors. Hence, every American Desi family we knew was in the same boat, challenging and enhancing their offspring's academic skills. On this day, Ronak's five more minutes of TV morphed into an hour; but at last, he mechanically completed his Kumon homework as quickly as he could.

Later, we made the ten-minute drive to the movie theater. While Neeraj bought the tickets, Ronak and I happily ordered popcorn, a hot dog, and some sweet-and-sour candies before stopping by the condiment stand to pour heaps of butter and salt on the tub of popcorn. That was my second favorite part of a movie theater experience. Even after thirteen years, I still missed the Indian style of eating Punjabi *samosas* at the movies. So, I compensated for the oily *samosas* with loads of butter on my popcorn. It didn't matter if the movie was good or bad; salty, warm, buttery popcorn in a big tub made it a complete movie experience for Neeraj and me, while Ronak was content with candy and a hot dog.

We thoroughly enjoyed the Narnia film without worrying about age-appropriate content, as it was a Disney movie.

We returned home by nine p.m. in a relaxed and happy mood; after this eventful and fulfilling weekend of family time, like runners, we turned our attention toward getting ready for yet another sprint—a busy and activity-oriented week ahead. In addition, it was time to approach the shipping companies about shipping our moving boxes to India—bringing us one step closer to our life-changing journey.

ோ

3

So, Why Move?

Why did I want to move, really? During the course of our journey, I often asked myself this question. Was it because I was tired of my relaxed suburban life in America and instead, craved a rich city life in Asia? Or did I just miss Mumbai?

The name of your birthplace, it is said, is permanently etched in your heart. I did have many logical and well-reasoned arguments in favor of our move back to our homeland, but Mumbai was engraved in my heart, which is why my feelings about Mumbai extended beyond the analytical and into the emotional.

Mumbai's appeal is manifold: a melting pot of India, Mumbai is the most easygoing city in India, making everyone feel socially included and welcomed. It is also a fast-paced metropolis, recognized as a fashion and economic capital, and a center for the Bollywood film industry. Yet, for me, it's the city of my childhood memories. For example, the Fort area reminds me of the telephone exchange office where my mom worked, a tall building near Flora Fountain. Sometimes, Mom took me with her if she went just to do some paperwork or for a half day, and on the way back, we would stop at the iconic Kamat's Restaurant in Fort for spicy *bhel puri* and delicious *dahi vada*. More than the food, though, I remember enjoying my mom's undivided attention, as it was just the two of us together at the table.

I also visited Mumbai's museum with my mom, while Azad Maidan reminds me of our many expeditions during the yearly Handloom Exhibition, when the sports grounds were transformed into an exhibition center. Mom would buy beautiful, vibrantly-colored woven crafts directly from weavers who came from all over India for the event. Mumbai memories with my dad include visiting Rajabai Tower when I accompanied him to Bombay University.

But of all Mumbai's many jewels, it is the beaches, especially Chowpatty and Juhu, that mean the most to me, a love sealed in childhood. Every summer and Diwali school vacation, Mom took my sisters and me, along with our cousins, to Juhu Beach, even though it meant taking us all by herself if Dad was busy. In those days, Mumbai beaches boasted elephants, horses, and camels, and their owners offered animal rides to paying customers. Mom believed that the strong camel scent improved the immune system, so we kids were allowed rides on all three animals. Afterward, we always impatiently visited the stalls for spicy snacks like *bhel puri* and *pani puri*, along with *gola* (shaved ice balls in colorful sherbet).

As soon as our eyes spied the churning sea waves, we would dash off to wade in them, leaving Mom in charge of our abandoned footwear, only to return fully drenched in seawater. Then, while we perched in the sand to dry ourselves, we cheerfully indulged in warm roasted corn fresh off the charcoal grill, smothered in salt-chili powder and lime juice. I cherished quiet moments admiring the sunsets beyond the sea line before we returned home refreshed.

In addition to its cultural sites and beaches, Mumbai has always been a secular city where people of all faiths and religions lived together and shared equal respect for all religions. Individuals of other religions would visit the public Hindu Ganapati Festival celebrations with great devotion. Similarly, my *aaji* (grandma) took us kids to the Mount Mary Church Fair celebration, or sometimes, my maternal uncle would take us, with equal devotion, to the Haji Malang Dargah, perched atop a mountain in Kalyan.

I definitely missed Mumbai's beaches and public festivals while living in America. But was I also tired of laid-back suburban American life? Was that at least a partial motivation for the "big move"?

I grew up listening to friends and extended family glorifying the U.S. In the 90s, people endlessly admired and praised this country, appreciating America for its lifestyle, standard of living, availability of higher education, and job opportunities. But, unlike the majority, my family never shared the public's fascination for the U.S., probably because my mom comes from a family of freedom fighters. Her father was a freedom fighter, and from the age of fifteen, devoted his life to the movement for Indian independence from Britain. Post-independence, beginning in 1947, he fought for postal workers' rights as a union leader. So, the respect for freedom fighters was deeply ingrained in us, and Mom always said one could accomplish anything in one's motherland.

I came to America only after my marriage and followed my husband, who happened to have an outstanding career with a decent salary in the U.S. Once here, I began learning about life in a rich country compared to a developing country. That helped me realize why people in my past were so fascinated by the U.S. I liked the ease and effortlessness of life in America, such as high-standard quality control on all consumer products, multiple personal and professional opportunities, and the excellent balance of family and work life. In America, one could efficiently devote time to the family while still maintaining a demanding career—you didn't have to choose one over the other.

After living in the U.S. for some time, when I would visit India for four weeks of vacation almost every year, I criticized the inadequacy of India's infrastructure, the inconvenience at the airport, especially their lack of concern for the passengers at the airport, or how much more crowded the city looked each year with an increasing population. Yet, while welcoming spring every year, I longed to visit India during the summer. I even sacrificed my long-standing dream of studying for an MBA at the University of Colorado–Denver when Neeraj pointed out that I couldn't make my yearly visit to India if I were studying for an MBA.

I was hell-bent on visiting India; I firmly believed that I should at least give my parents the happiness of seeing their daughter once a year. Besides, I genuinely feel that every one of us is searching for a comfortable, amicable solution for keeping everyone happy—something that works like a hearty soup, elevating your mood and spirit and filling your heart in your everyday life. Time spent in India soothed my soul as nothing else could, a warmth and gratification I first discovered in childhood. From my earliest memories, I had always felt the activity, fervor, affection, and bubbly conversations that defined a house full of multigenerational family members. This bustle was so natural, so well-orchestrated, that I couldn't identify one specific moment when I became an inseparable part of the family and the home—it was just always there, around me and within me.

My childhood had been idyllic. I grew up under Mom and Dad's loving wings with two sisters, uncles, an aunt, and a full-time maid. My grandparents also occasionally visited us from our native region for a month or two. If our parents were upset with us for some reason, I always found myself sheltered by my uncles or aunt. It felt very comforting to have so many people in the house who cared for me, answered my questions, and helped me with homework or craft assignments. After my uncles and aunt got married, our family became a nuclear family of five. Our festivals still remained joyous with heartwarming family gatherings when they visited with their respective families. Memories of colorful festivals full of happiness and love, shared with our extended family, always make me nostalgic.

Sometimes during summer breaks from school, my *aaji* or my maternal uncle took me to Mom's village in Konkan; sitting in the window seat of the semi-luxury bus, I would hum my favorite songs on that eight-to-nine-hour journey, both enjoying and curiously observing the ever-changing landscapes and the hilly slopes of the beautifully diverse Western Ghats. Upon reaching Mom's ancestral homeland, I knew I could go to any neighboring house and be welcomed just like family. The residents knew my parents and grandparents well; some were even distant relatives of ours. A typical evening meal we enjoyed beneath dim lantern lights would be *rotis* and *pithi* (powdered horse-gram curry) cooked in a terra-cotta pot on the wood-burning stove, accompanied by roasted dried fish.

Konkan is known for its natural beauty, peace, and tranquility. The lack of automation in the region was well compensated for by clean air and sweet-tasting water from the wells. An abundance of exotic fruits and nuts, such as jackfruits, cashews, and world-famous Alphonso mangoes, was easily found in one's backyard. And jumping from house to house and eating mangoes on those scorching summer afternoons stayed with me for a long time.

The cashew and mango trees in my aaji's *backyard always transport me back to my childhood.*

It's no surprise that I wanted my child to experience that same fun with extended family, along with the warmth and celebration of our culture and its diverse essence. I had hoped for Ronak to learn about his roots before he faced the world independently. Also, I wanted him to experience playtime that took place spontaneously and unsupervised by parents, unlike the preplanned playdates I scheduled with his friends in Denver. Outside the U.S., things might be different; he might have to face other life challenges and work harder than usual. But I believed it would shape him into a tenacious, determined person.

Yet many people didn't understand.

One of my close friends, Kruti, asked, "Why are you going back after so many years of residency here?"

"I feel my son should know his roots," I said.

"But every year, you spend three to four weeks of summer vacation in India, right?" she scoffed.

"My dear, our kids get the undivided attention of all our relatives in those three or four weeks, so it's not much of a learning experience. Besides, my child can't truly understand India until he lives there as a resident rather than a visitor." My convictions remained firm, no matter how intensely I was challenged.

I came to a more profound realization of this after my dad passed away when Ronak was still so young. I wanted Ronak, as an only child, to live closer to his relatives, who were mostly Mumbai-based, so he could be close to extended family in his growing years.

"But he grew up here. Will he adjust there?" Kruti sounded genuinely concerned.

"Yes, that will be pivotal, our prime effort. If he doesn't, we will not hesitate to return to the U.S."

But even Neeraj expressed some doubts. "Why are you so keen on going to India?"

"It's our home, after all. And why are you asking me that after thirteen years of marriage?" I growled at him. At the time of our wedding, we had talked about returning to India. That had been my only condition before marriage, to which Neeraj had readily agreed.

"Things change over time, and I thought maybe just a vacation to India would be enough for you now," he answered sheepishly.

"Are we moving only for me? Don't you want to go?" I unleashed my frustration. "And what about Ronak? Don't you want him to enjoy the same experiences we had growing up?"

"No . . . I don't mean that . . ." Neeraj offered reluctantly.

"Okay. Then let's talk about the issues."

"Well, professionally, it's going to be challenging finding a good source of income and jobs to our liking."

"Well, we keep hearing that many offshore developments are being sent to India nowadays. Why would experienced people like us not find job opportunities of our choice over there?" I was shooting blanks with no proper groundwork at that point. I added, "I believe employers will be lining up for us; think how we can serve as an interface, bridging the gap between countries."

Neeraj remained silent, appearing unenthusiastic.

I was determined to compromise. "Neeraj, if that is a concern, we could start looking for jobs now, line up interviews with prospective companies around summertime, and see how it goes and where it takes us."

Neeraj only nodded. I imagined he was probably lost in his thoughts as he tried to process jobs overseas, interviews with Indian companies, and similar scenarios. "Maybe we should try something like my friend Jeevan did," he offered.

I listened attentively, as this was the first time Neeraj had been vocal about this issue.

Neeraj continued, "Jeevan quit his job in Texas and looked for an appropriate company within America that was interested in expansion overseas. Finally, he found one based in Silicon Valley."

"I remember Jeevan. They left Texas a while ago, but only moved to India last year, right?" I vaguely recalled.

"Yes, that was his strategic job move before they moved to India; they worked in California for two years with the same company."

"Wow, that's very long-term planning! I—"

Neeraj cut off my sentence as he turned to leave and said, "We should start planning now for something like bringing the job to India, or maybe helping an American company expand their operations in India."

I immediately wondered, *But would they give us the city of our choice?* However, I bit my tongue, telling myself, *You can't have everything; you might get the move to India but might not get the town you prefer.* The answer sounded exactly like what Neeraj would say had I voiced my opinion. He was more open to going wherever the job took him, even in India, and I appreciated that he was more aware of and sensitive to the potential challenges of life in India. I knew I could always count on him for his pragmatism.

4

Preparation: So Much to Do

Where, When, and How

The logistics of the move were complicated and many-layered. In the past, I was challenged by a chicken-and-egg puzzle in my mind. Whenever I thought about moving to India, I always held back this idea, as we did not own property there. So, our move was constantly put off and never pursued.

To begin with, we would need a roof over our heads. After living on our own for thirteen years in the U.S., to expect our parents to house us long-term would have been outlandish. We were also used to having our lifestyle and surroundings a certain way. So, the question became, where will we live in India?

Because both Neeraj and I were born and raised in Mumbai, we unanimously decided to make that our destination. As a first step toward the move, in 2005, we began exploring the housing options well in advance of our move year. We knew that once we bought a suitable under-construction apartment in Mumbai, it would take a very long time for it to be move-in ready. Our search criteria were based on new construction projects and the cost of the apartments. We had multiple options to consider.

There were NRI (non-resident Indian) colonies available in India with certain luxuries and amenities. These apartments had a reasonable quota of help, recreational facilities within the complex, and were predominantly occupied by returning NRIs and expats.

There were also 'tower' projects: skyscrapers that featured lavish apartments for Indian nationals and foreigners.

In addition, we needed school areas that catered to upper-middle-class families.

Considering Ronak's age, an apartment with recreational facilities like a tennis court, swimming pool, soccer field, or at least a small playground for bouncing a ball was desirable.

Then again, hoping to be in regular contact with relatives, we wanted to reside in the center of Mumbai.

Moreover, Ronak had visited Mumbai every summer since he was a year old, and since Juhu Beach was his favorite destination, we also aspired to buy an apartment there.

Because we hadn't lived in Mumbai in the last thirteen years, to fully understand the current system and the ins and outs of the present lifestyle, we needed guidance from our family. And who better than the person who held my hand in my childhood and taught me how to walk—my mom. Living close to her would be invaluable.

When we researched and visited the apartment projects in Mumbai, we were taken aback by the city's expensive real estate market. As we explored Juhu, considering the area's socioeconomic culture, high cost of apartments, and, most importantly, traffic issues, we decided to look into a newly developing area instead.

This area was part of the Western suburbs, with lots of open space nearby and easy access to the highways, and it was away from the chaos of main thoroughfares like SV Road and Link Road. Located in a business area, it had an excellent system for keeping it clean.

The cherry on top was that, while it was secluded from the regular roads and blocked entirely on one side by a creek, this was a tranquil neighborhood. The builder informed us that the surrounding schools catered to the upper middle class. The apartment was a two-bedroom and would be available in the next two years after the construction phase was complete. Finally, on completion, in 2008, my mom and sisters took the keys on our behalf.

Having achieved one of our main objectives—securing a place to live in Mumbai—ignited our decision to move back and work toward the ultimate goal of relocating.

Jobs and School

Happy to have found a place to live, we now turned our attention to our next goals: jobs and Ronak's education.

Following the insightful conversation that we'd had about jobs, Neeraj and I both began searching for employers with offshore projects. Neeraj expressed that it was relatively easy to adjust socio-economically, but job satisfaction and a good work environment could not be compromised, so those factors were essential to us.

We kept looking for opportunities but to no avail. Still, we were committed to moving before Ronak turned eleven because after that, the transition would have been much more difficult for him. So, the move date was tentatively set for May 2009, as the next school year in India would begin in June.

We had to prepare for the move accordingly. Above all, we had three important tasks ahead of us: first, to find suitable jobs; second, to secure Ronak's Mumbai school admission for the next academic year; and last, if we secured his school admission but didn't find jobs by that time, then we still would have to move before Ronak's Indian school year began in June. We were in a dilemma. We had to support ourselves financially but also had to start Ronak's schooling without disrupting his academic schedule. So, keeping everything in perspective and the final goal in mind, I decided to quit my job to prepare for the move and make the completion of Ronak's school admission a priority. I was okay with not focusing on my career then and wanted to focus entirely on motherhood duties. I had no better role model than my own mother.

During my primary and middle school years, Mom always took a whole month off from work to prep us, kids, for our finals. Of course, being a mother of three, she barely had any vacation time left in those days, yet she took that month off without pay to prepare us, sacrificing an entire month's salary every year in hopes of her children's positive report cards. Following her example, choosing my child over a job was an easy decision. Neeraj also supported my choice, as one of us would have to manage Ronak's world, while the other worked until we found a long-term dual-career solution.

We knew that we would not be walking on a golden carpet in India. This adventure would have its challenges, but life would be agreeable if we stayed true to our reasons instead of expecting too much of everything. If we were clear about our motivation for moving, then not having luxury cars, excess space in our home, or a big backyard with flowerbeds and fruit trees wouldn't matter much.

Soon, I would have to complete Ronak's school admission during my mini trip with Ronak to India in February 2009. However, our job search remained challenging, as the first quarter of 2009 passed without any leads. The second quarter finally arrived, and in the middle of it was our moving date, but we had yet to discover any viable job opportunities. This directed us toward the other important decision we had to make.

Over the years, we learned from a few of our acquaintances in America that they had also tried moving back to India in the past, but ultimately, had abandoned their plans when they could not find jobs in India when applying from the U.S. Fearing we might end up disconsolate like them, we decided that I would take Ronak to India to start the school year on the actual moving date, in May 2009, and later, look for a job while protecting Ronak's world and finding our footing in the new country. Neeraj would continue to work in the U.S. to support our family financially during that stage. Simultaneously, he would also continue his job search in India from the U.S. while wrapping up his remaining tasks; then after about six months, he would join us in India. It was a very odd decision, but we were still searching for solutions to our self-imposed puzzle.

We were also worried about the impact on our finances if we weren't able to find appropriate jobs in India. We had no clear picture of the job market there. Still, we were dedicated to moving before Ronak turned eleven. And, worst-case scenario, if things didn't work out in India, we had complete faith in our ability to return and start over in the U.S.

5

Mumbai School Admission

Having quit my job, I now turned my attention to our next priority: Ronak's education. Concerned about school admissions before the move, I traveled with Ronak to Mumbai in February 2009 to check out a few schools for the following academic year. I was surprised to learn that there was no uniform school curriculum in Mumbai. Instead, various educational boards coexisted in the city:

SSC (Secondary School Certificate—Maharashtra State Board)

CBSE (Central Board of Secondary Education)

ICSE (Indian Certificate of Secondary Education—this existed across India)

IGCSE (International General Certificate of Secondary Education)

IB (International Baccalaureate, a program based in Switzerland)

I was frankly perplexed by this assortment. Growing up, I had only known the state educational system (SSC board) that I studied.

"And look how wonderfully we've turned out," Neeraj argued over the phone.

"But we don't know if we might have to move within India for a job. In that case, ICSE or CBSE could be more practical." I tried to simplify the information overload.

"Okay, do they have a presence across India?" Neeraj asked.

"CBSE is more focused in the South, but ICSE is relatively widespread."

"Then it's simple; go with ICSE."

"But I hear it's tougher than SSC," I warned.

Based on word of mouth and the school preferences of a few acquaintances in my mom's neighborhood, I had short-listed three schools before leaving home. I had spoken by phone with one international ICSE school's principal that week. Mrs. Irawati was kind enough to meet me for an in-person chat. It was the first time as a parent that I would meet an Indian school principal and see the school from the inside. I reached the building gate before our scheduled appointment time, but the surroundings looked deserted, as the school day was over. As soon as I entered the gate, my eyes met a small, stunning, polished white marble temple perched on a pedestal at the school entrance; inside the temple, a picture-perfect white marble Saraswati idol (Goddess of knowledge) subtly smiled. Mesmerized by this beauty, I folded my hands with devotion.

A few steps into the building, it felt like the place was screaming for a makeover. It was the first school I had visited in India in many years, so I was unsure whether this was typical or perhaps this school was an exception.

As I climbed the stairs to the office, the stairway seemed dark, and I wondered if they were trying to save on the cost of lightbulbs. The color of the interior was barely visible in some parts of the building. At the front desk, the office staff completely disregarded me and continued working. I informed one of the personnel who briefly gave me her attention that I had an appointment with the principal. She showed me four empty chairs, which constituted their waiting area. I took a seat while the staff ignored me for the next twenty minutes. I grew anxious and reminded them about the meeting.

"Ma'am is busy; we will call you," one of the people behind the desk answered without even looking at me.

I was determined to find the right school for Ronak, so I kept calm.

As I finally entered the principal's office, Mrs. Irawati reached across the desk to shake my hand. I guessed her to be a little over fifty. She looked fit for her age.

"I'm looking to enroll my son in the fifth grade," I said.

"Which school are you coming from?"

"From a school in America, but we will be moving here in three months."

As we conversed, she explained about the twenty-five-to-one student-to-teacher ratio in each class, and most notably, that they had only one division per class. I was thrilled by the small class size, which meant each student would likely be known by name rather than becoming just another face in the crowd. She also shared proudly that the results from their tenth-grade ICSE board examination were 100 percent. Tenth board results in India were crucial in deciding students' career path choices. Nevertheless, I wanted to address the school's outdated look. As though reading my mind, leaning back in her chair, she said, "We will be moving to a new school building in December 2009."

New building? Great. That should look so much better, I thought. But if they were moving too far from this area, conveniently located near my new apartment, we might have to look for another school.

"The new building is only six traffic lights away in Malad." Again, she must have read my mind. To my astonishment, this school featured a traditional school system, so I quickly requested the admission form. When she mentioned wanting to meet the student before his admission, we set up a meeting with Ronak the following week.

When I visited my second choice, an international school that offered the IGCSE and ICSE systems, they arranged an official school tour. I was pleased to see that their educational approach was somewhat similar to that of Ronak's school in the U.S. It seemed like an up-to-date school with state-of-the-art real estate and more facilities, but they charged a nonrefundable fee of Rs 20,000 (Indian rupees) just for the admission form. It amounted to approximately $416 in 2009; however, keeping Ronak in mind, I paid it without hesitation. But then, in a new-admission orientation meeting for parents, I learned that they painted a very rosy picture of their institution, while the school's principal intentionally dodged the questions parents asked. In the end, the school promoted only IGCSE enrollment, and I was not sure how long this foreign concept would last in India, so we moved on from that school.

The third facility, also an IGCSE school, seemed newly built, with the bonus feature of a beautiful playground on the premises. During an interview with the coordinator, I learned about their policy of allowing only vegetarian school lunches.

"Really?" I asked incredulously.

"We don't allow non-vegetarian items on the lunch menu, as

most of our management is from the vegetarian community." Mrs. Chandani smirked.

"But I can send a lunch box from home with my son, right?" I frowned.

Lunchables with turkey and cheese slices were my last-minute resort for super-busy Monday mornings. The rest of the week, Ronak's favorite dinosaur-shaped chicken nuggets or chicken sausages were the only bait I could include in a lunch box to encourage him to take at least a few bites of his lunch. I wondered what he would eat if it were a vegetarian lunch box.

"Unfortunately, our strict policy doesn't allow non-veg food in a lunch box." Mrs. Chandani seemed irritated.

I had short-listed only a few schools, and if the others didn't come through, I needed to keep this one as part of my contingency plan. So, instead of reacting, I requested the admission form.

"That will be fifteen hundred rupees." It was approximately $31 in 2009. Mrs. Chandani happily handed me the paperwork.

Finally, after a week, I took Ronak to school number one for an appointment with Principal Irawati. In my research, I had read and heard from other cautious parents about the basics of school admissions in India.

"There is already so much competition because of the population growth in this country, and it adds pressure on the kids," my friend Sunita had cautioned me.

"At the same time, the school authorities are expecting kids to be more disciplined at a much younger age," my mom's neighbor added.

"Ronak, answer only what you are asked," I instructed as I unruffled his hair on our way to the school.

Arriving before our meeting time, I observed Ronak as we

walked through the school gate and into a dark, empty corridor with colorless walls. My son displayed no outward emotion, and I thought he was very courageous. Only a handful of people were on-site, as it was a half-day session. At the school office, I stood quietly at the office window, per my American expectations, waiting to hear, "How may I help you?" I waited patiently for five minutes before addressing the clerk who had spoken to me last time.

"She's busy. You should wait," she suggested.

Ronak remained silent during this conversation. Finally, we got the green light to meet the principal. As I held Ronak's hand and looked into his eyes, I nodded to reassure him. "Are you ready?" A silly question, perhaps. Looking a little overwhelmed, he just nodded.

After knocking on the door, we entered the office gingerly. Mrs. Irawati pointed at the chairs in front of her desk and asked us to sit down. She seemed very vigilant, watching our every move. Draped in a vibrant orange-and-white *saree* with a red *bindi* on her forehead, she looked graceful. After staring at the colorless corridor walls for the past fifteen minutes, I found her *saree* colors refreshing.

She dove right in, bypassing any small talk, and asked Ronak directly about his favorite subjects, explicitly focusing on his mathematics, English, and science scores. Ronak answered confidently, and I sighed with relief. However, Mrs. Irawati's next statement reignited my anxiety. She suggested that Ronak take the English and mathematics tests in the next room while she interviewed me. Quite stunned to hear that he had to take a test immediately, Ronak turned his head and looked right at me, while I looked incredulously at the principal. I was a little irked by the lack of preparation time. I grimaced apologetically at Ronak but pulled myself together and directed him to take the test.

We were led to the room, which was more of a back room to the principal's office, equipped with a midsize table and four chairs. An office staff member instantly appeared with the test papers and set some pens and a pencil on the table. Ronak sat there quietly before reluctantly picking up a pen.

"I'm right here, Ronak. They said it's a concise test," I offered, trying to boost his morale. His face showed surprise, and although I could tell he was disheartened, he began writing.

I returned to the principal's office to continue our interview. Mrs. Irawati asked about our background and why we were leaving the U.S. She described her school again and emphasized how they always achieved a 100 percent passing score in the tenth-grade ICSE board results by putting extra effort into each student's academic growth from ninth grade onward. Her eyes brimmed with pride when she said that most students got above 85 percent on their tenth-grade results. Mrs. Irawati struck me as a disciplinarian who strived to provide an academically inspired environment for all her students.

After the test, she approved Ronak's admission to their school.

"Finally!" I sighed, and we paid the fees and submitted the admission form to the office. I also asked about the paperwork and certificates required for international transfer. I felt that all the teachers and principals I had talked to up to that point had been very cooperative in sharing any information I'd requested. But the school's office staff, appointed to provide information to students, remained stone-faced and, with their dry nature, made the information-seeking person, in this case, me, feel subjugated before parting with any information. Still, I chose to focus on the positive. *We've found a good school for Ronak. Another step closer to our goal of moving back to India.*

᚛

6

Mixed Reactions to Our Move

With Ronak's school admission secured and our Mumbai residence ready, we felt prepared to move. The plan was to leave Denver at the end of the American academic year and reach India a week before Mumbai schools opened for the next academic year, around June 7th, so we'd have at least seven days to prepare before the first day of school. My plan for our first six months in India was to focus solely on Ronak's adjustment, since everything would be new for him, especially academically. Once he was comfortably settled, I would apply for a job.

In the meantime, we finally told our Colorado friends and colleagues about our moving date. People were used to hearing the word "move," since many often moved within the U.S. for work or other reasons. Still, as our friends got their heads around the concept of our move, they were blue. But the addition of "to India" elicited responses ranging from shock and surprise to upset and even amusement. I vividly remember many different reactions.

"How can you renounce everything and move to India so suddenly? I'm very angry with you," my friend Richa said.

Considering we'd been friends for several years, I knew she spoke out of love and her distress over losing a friend to a different country. Later, she arranged a potluck get-together for us with a dozen families, all our friends. They cooked delicious food and gave us a piece of Swarovski crystal as a farewell gift.

My North Indian friends from work similarly expressed their shock. "What are you going back to and for?" they questioned in the same tone. But they, too, lovingly invited us for a send-off dinner party. Even so, the dinner table conversation was interrogative.

Shamita voiced her reservations. "So, what are you going to do? It's not easy there, workwise. And environmentally, the city is so polluted."

So many questions, but our answer was always the same: "We will see."

We were determined to make it despite all the negativity we heard. Our visits to Mumbai for the past thirteen summers assured us that Ronak had seen the city and felt comfortable there. And it seemed absurd that people had so many doubts on our behalf when we felt cautiously optimistic.

My group of friends from the day I first landed in the U.S.—my husband's work buddies' spouses—gathered at the home of my dear friend, Geeta. We reminisced, sharing sentimental memories from our early days in America. They thoughtfully gave us gift cards to purchase the things we would need for our Indian apartment.

Around that time, the movie *Slumdog Millionaire*[1] was making waves in theaters. Shot in Asia's biggest slum, Dharavi, it attracted more attention to the city of Mumbai. Spoiler alert: Dharavi is only a small part of Mumbai; it's not the entire city. Some elements of the film focus on the living conditions in the Dharavi slums, but not everyone understood that. One of our very close American family friends kindly invited us for a bon voyage dinner, where they affectionately expressed how much they would miss us. But suddenly, the wife asked, "Why are you taking Ronak to that Mumbai?"

I was taken aback. "What do you mean by 'that Mumbai'?"

"The Mumbai we saw in that movie concerned us," she said, "and I'm worried about Ronak. Why don't you both go ahead but leave Ronak here? He can stay with us and complete his education here."

We were touched by her concern and willingness to offer her home to Ronak for the sake of his education.

"We appreciate the offer, but the slum is only one part of Mumbai, not the whole of Mumbai," I clarified, hoping to put her mind at ease. "We will be living in a skyscraper, which will have half the space we are used to enjoying here but will provide most of the amenities we need."

In fact, even some of my relatives in Mumbai had similar concerns, but they seldom expressed them directly. Some of their thoughts were, "Maybe Neeraj and Hemangi are not doing well at their jobs," and, "Perhaps the American economy distresses them." In reality, we both had well-paying jobs. I had resigned from my position at Comcast to prepare for the move.

"We hear the American economy is down, and now that you are back in India, how can you afford this latest cell phone model?" one of my aunts asked, ogling my pink Motorola phone after we arrived in India. I was speechless.

Even my own mom expressed some doubts. When I shared our decision to move, she asked, "Why do you want to move back after you have settled there with your family? Why change?"

I didn't enjoy the constant doubts and questions from family and friends in both India and the U.S., though I did appreciate their concern. But the more I replied to their questions and comments, the stronger my conviction became.

ℭℛ

7

Ronak's Response

Before leaving Colorado, we were swamped with many decisions—selling our cars, listing furniture for sale online, staging a garage sale to unload trivial items, deciding on our shipments, packing our bags, and procuring our medical records and educational transcripts to bring with us to India. But Ronak got a little quieter and more introspective than usual in those days, with his face showing subtle signs of worry. I tried to fend off his sad feelings by doing my best not to make it apparent that we were uprooting our base and moving to a different country. Neeraj and I packed either in the basement or in the upstairs bedrooms while Ronak watched TV in the family room. The rest of it we packed while he was asleep.

Toward the last two weeks of his fourth grade, I started preparing him for the move. I explained that, soon, we would leave for India, but after fourth grade, most of his friends would move on from their primary school anyway. Although a few might stay at the same school, many would opt for different schools. This put a temporary bandage on his aching heart for his friends and set his mind at ease—or so we thought.

At the same time, we went full throttle with Ronak's Hindi language lessons. When I first interviewed at the Mumbai schools, I learned that those students had been learning Hindi since third grade. Ronak would be joining them in fifth grade. His progress was impressive over the past two months, considering he was learning the Hindi alphabet for the first time in his life. Nevertheless, I noticed that his innocent face sometimes reflected the questions in his mind, and it tore at my heart. Other than that, he seemed to handle this news very well—or so we thought.

One afternoon, ten days before our departure, Neeraj and I were clearing out the garage while Ronak rode his mountain bike in our neighborhood. Our house was situated at the bottom of a slope. My neighbor called and said Ronak had fallen off his bike. Apparently, he had hit the brake hard and flipped the bike while coming down the road, falling near the fourth house from ours. We rushed out to find Ronak's right hand wounded, his forehead bruised, and his knee and elbow scraped and bloody. We were so thankful that his helmet had protected him. Sniffling, he tried to lift his bike, but Neeraj ran and picked him up, rushing him to our house.

Once home, we tried to stop the bleeding with ice and cotton and gave Ronak water as we wiped his tears. But when he saw the blood-soaked cotton balls, the floodgates opened, and he cried in earnest. It seemed as if all the pain and suppressed questions and emotions now surfaced in the form of tears. I swallowed a lump in my throat and looked at Neeraj, whose tight face also showed tension. We rushed Ronak to urgent care, where, suspecting a hairline fracture, they put his hand in a sling and assured us he'd be fine.

That night, we engaged Ronak in a casual chat in hopes he'd open up to us. After evading several questions, he pressed his face to my shoulder and wept, saying for the first time, "I don't want to leave Colorado."

It tore our hearts out to see his innocent, petrified face, full of questions about the unseen and the unknown. Feeling deeply rattled, we instantly caved.

"Let's forget it. We can cancel," Neeraj offered with his eyes welling up. "Even though we sold the furniture, our house is still intact. We can always buy new furniture and cancel the airline tickets."

Later, I wrapped my arms around Ronak and, tucking him in his bed, assured him, "We won't move if you're scared. But, Ronak, before you decide, let's think about this." I wanted him to understand. "In India, you will see Grandma all the time, and you will get lots of school days off, especially in the rainy season."

"But I get my snow days off here too," he whispered.

"Yes, but here, we have only six long weekends. In India, they have many, many festivals and just as many holidays! Think about it?"

Then Neeraj added an essential piece to the conversation. "What if we go to India as planned, and then, if we don't like living there after a year, we come back here?"

That thought seemed to help Ronak relax, and he drifted off to sleep. Neeraj and I remained shaken but determined to do the best for our son.

Goodbye, Colorado!

We said goodbye to our Denver house.

In the weeks before our departure, we had prepared a separate adventure as a surprise gift for Ronak. Our Disney World vacation was a well-deserved gift for him, considering he would lose his summer vacation in the U.S. and get only seven days in India before starting school in Mumbai.

We planned and obtained our air tickets, hotel reservations, and Disney World tickets so we could enjoy five relaxed days of family vacation before Ronak and I flew to India with our one-way tickets and Neeraj returned to work in Colorado.

The day we left Colorado, my feelings were mixed. Of course, I longed to see our move to India become a reality, but I was also saying goodbye to a home I had loved. And I was achingly aware of the many wrapping-up tasks that remained incomplete.

Before closing the door for the final time, I touched the house's walls and hugged our remaining furniture goodbye. I knew I would miss my expansive kitchen, our backyard, the trees, and our walk-in closet, which was mostly occupied with my clothes. I stepped onto the deck to gaze across our backyard with all the trees and then closed my eyes to sear those images into my memory banks. We also reminded Ronak to bid goodbye to the house. Even with the Disney World theme playing in his head, he was quiet but conducted himself well and did not appear too distraught. However, when he hugged the big wall in the living room and lovingly touched our tall tree in the yard, none of us could hide our tears.

Nine years earlier, when we had built this new house, like kids in a candy store at the design center, we had excitedly chosen the exterior color, flooring, carpet, granite, and cabinets. Ronak was just a toddler then. We had spent nine whole years in this house, enjoying prosperity, happiness, and growth. We stepped out of the house with heavy luggage and heavier hearts while my mind swirled with memories.

Our sadness at leaving was softened by our excitement over the family vacation. Except for a few mood swings during the first two days, Ronak seemed fine focusing on Disney World, and planning which theme park to visit first.

Over the next five days, our vacation elevated our mood. Ronak had to wear a sling to keep his injured hand secured throughout the trip, but that never stopped him from becoming utterly immersed in that magical experience.

For Ronak, Disney World was a dream come true. In spite of his initial sadness, he was ecstatic once we arrived, particularly after visiting the Animal Kingdom theme park. To him, walking on Tarzan's timber bridge with a grin on his face, adventurously climbing Tarzan's rope ladders, then excitedly taking a boat safari on an island and spying a gorilla habitat was like finding a hidden treasure. Locked in my memory forever will be the priceless, delighted look on my son's face. That enchanted look on Ronak's face scored number one when compared to our entire magical vacation. The worries he had shown evaporated into thin air, and it was hard to believe he was the same boy who had flipped his bicycle only a few days earlier. I thought, *With so many challenges finally behind us, we're beginning our journey in the best frame of mind.*

Once Ronak and I were settled on our fourteen-hour flight to Mumbai, Ronak seemed interested in the onboard movie selections after our meals, so I quietly opened my diary, which I had been using to plan this move, and checked a few items off my to-do list.

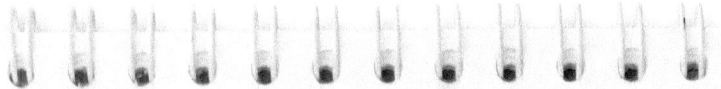

Hem's List

Before the Move

- Pack boxes before departure   **✗**
  (Relying on Neeraj to finish the rest
  while he's still in Denver.)

- Sell furniture   **✓**
  (Mostly sold except the cars and
  essential furniture for Neeraj.)

- Pack personal bags   *almost done*
  (The things we could fit in, we did;
  the rest, Neeraj will either ship or
  bring later.)

- Prepare Ronak for the move   *ongoing*

- Pick up family medical records   **✓**

- Interview school principals before   **✓**
  admission applications

- Complete school admission   **✓**

- Teach Ronak Hindi   *ongoing*

Postmove Projects

- Hire household help in Mumbai *(hopeful)*
- Hire home cook *(hopeful)*
- Hire driver *(once we buy our car)*
- Get custom-made furniture *(dreaming every day)*
- Have colorful apartment walls *(dreaming every day)*
- Swing by Mom's apartment
  anytime *(Sounds like music to my ears!)*
- Visit extended family *(Plan to do it once a quarter)*

ℭℛ

PART TWO

Transitioning to Mumbai

8

Excited! We Landed

I boarded this plane knowing our one-way tickets would soon seal the deal and officially mark us as residents of India—there was no going back now on our decision to move. With bittersweet emotions, we finally concluded our journey, landing in Mumbai at midnight after fourteen hours on our last flight. My mind slowly grasped that we were in our homeland now; I was in no hurry to collect our luggage. Strolling slowly with Ronak, I watched other people rushing toward the immigration counters. After the crowd scattered toward the exit, we reached the baggage claim. I eventually grabbed our checked luggage from the carousel while Ronak kept an eye on our carry-on bags. I felt exhausted after thirteen years of dreaming about the move and twenty-eight hours of travel. I was happy and relieved to have come this far, but my heart was heavy for having left Neeraj behind in America.

It was still dark, but outside the terminal, the floodlights made everything look bright. We immediately felt the heat and humidity as we boarded the oversized taxi that I had booked in advance to accommodate not only our mass of luggage but also my relatives, who'd arrived to meet us. Even at two forty-five a.m., the roads were busy with traffic, and exiting the highway, we saw a few hawkers sleeping on the sidewalk. The difference was stark; I rarely saw people out on the streets in Denver except in the summer months, but here in Mumbai, I saw a few sleeping along the road. When we left the main road for the side streets, I noticed a few people gathered around a street vendor selling ice cream. Coming from a suburban American town where everyone seemed to be in bed by ten p.m., I was now entering the suburbs of a Mumbai that rarely sleeps.

I grew more and more eager the closer we got to Mom's apartment. I couldn't wait to see her. My mom always seemed like a goddess equipped with several arms, effortlessly fighting demons, protecting the world, and blessing her devotees while revealing a subtle smile on her radiantly glowing face. Even as a working woman, Mom showered us with love and nurtured and cared for us tirelessly. She was always a very courageous, audacious individual. I vividly remember as a five-year-old walking with her toward our neighborhood during one monsoon afternoon. The rain had stopped; Mom closed her umbrella but chose to leave my raincoat on me. We walked, and from the corner of my eye, I was distracted by something glimmering in the sunlight. Several purple flowers glowed in a small pond beside the road. Although the water was covered in algae, some deep green leaves and lavender water-hyacinth flowers floated on the surface. Mesmerized, I sat on the concrete bench, sandwiched between the pond and the road. Mom joined me, and I asked her to get me one of those flowers. "We're late. We should go," she insisted.

As a five-year-old, I must have been very persuasive with my pout and please-please-please request. She thought for a moment, then acquiesced to my childish demand and went to the end of the concrete bench, and from its shallow corner, quickly stepped into the pond. However, the minute she left the road, I panicked and begged her to return, but by then, Mom had her feet submerged in the water and was laser-focused on picking the perfect flower for her daughter. I was awestruck, and to this day, I still get goosebumps remembering that incident. I admired her fearlessness and her love for me. Like a victorious warrior with an affectionate smile, she brought me a purple flower. At that instant, I no longer cared about the flower; instead, I hugged my mom tightly, relieved she was safe.

Hailing from a comfortable household and as a proud daughter of a freedom-fighter-cum-social-worker father and a strong-minded mother, Mom gave her all to our upbringing. She always cooked delicious yet nutritious meals for us while working as a central government employee, beginning as a telephone operator and eventually rising to a supervisor's position. In that capacity, she managed multiple young female staffers who worked as operators. She was considerate to those young women grappling with their responsibilities as new mothers and wives.

Although my mom had different work shifts, I was always around when she got ready for her nine-to-six shift. I remember Mom leaving for work in neatly draped and pinned *sarees* in chiffon, polyester, or silk. She complemented their vibrant colors with a matching barrette clipping her wavy black hair. Her watch on one wrist, gold bangles on the other, button-size gold earrings, a gold *mangalsutra* (black beaded necklace with a gold pendant), and a maroon *bindi* on her forehead completed her look. As a child, I checked her leather handbag just out of curiosity, only to find bus tickets, a train pass, a small money pouch, and some quick snacks—peanuts or raisins.

I was very fond of Mom's expensive silk *saree* collection in various weaves—Narayan Peth, Kanjeevaram, Patola, Bandhani, and Jijamata—to be worn for celebrations. Mom was never possessive about her beautiful *sarees*; if I ever asked to wear one, she would generously help me drape those gorgeous fabrics around myself.

Mom invested so much in us and our future. Without her initiative, my badminton, bicycle, classical vocal, and harmonium training would never have been possible. Her remaining salary was spent buying expensive nuts and dried fruits—considered luxuries in those days—for her growing children. In addition to our other hobbies and activities, Mom trained us in the art of *rangoli* to encourage our artistic side. I always loved putting this sand art outside our main door during the Diwali Festival. Before Diwali, she bought *rangoli* colors and design books and encouraged us to practice our craft.

Although I admired how hard she worked, I also loved the sense of warmth I felt when Mom stayed home. On the days she stayed home from work during my elementary school years, I would fake a stomachache or headache to stay home with her. I'm sure Mom knew I was faking it, but she still allowed me to miss school.

Contrary to the gender norms of the time, the 80s, our parents never required us to engage in housework just because we were girls. Mom always said that we'd have to cook once we got married, so she made sure we mastered the basics of cooking and could feed our future families, but in the meantime, we enjoyed her cooking while at home. I still lovingly recall the tangy taste of the *ragda* patties, *dahi vada*, and *pani puri* Mom prepared on Saturdays during summer vacations.

My parents always shielded us, kids, from adult arguments. They never had any significant arguments in front of us, and my father was particularly conscientious about maintaining a sound and supportive family environment. This led me to believe that once you reach your parents' age, you never quarrel; you learn to adjust.

Now, as I stood at Mom's doorstep, my childhood flashed before my eyes. Even though it was night, the apartment shone brightly in my memory. I pictured Mom sitting on the shaded swing chair facing the balcony on a sunny afternoon, overlooking the dense green mangroves and delighting in the fresh, cool breeze that wafted in from the creek.

On this night, as Mom, in a cotton *saree*, opened the door and welcomed us, her beautiful eyes were kind as always, and her serene smile looked youthful with a dimple. Her hair was gathered neatly in a clip at the nape of her neck, highlighting the gray streaks. Ronak and I hugged her immediately, and it was bliss. Embracing Mom epitomized the feeling that we were finally back home after all the preparation, planning, and scheduling that had dominated the past two years.

My mom and sister had lovingly decorated the living room with balloons, a "Welcome!" sign, and a cake for Ronak. It was a warm and beautiful welcome. Although joyful, we were exhausted after our twenty-eight-hour journey. I was grateful we'd be staying at Mom's while I got our Mumbai apartment move-in ready. With this sweet, feather-like feeling in my heart, I hit the bed and surrendered to sleep.

The next morning, Ronak woke me, and as I opened my eyes, I noticed the ceiling fan rotating at high speed and understood that our central-AC-habituated eyes and bodies would have to adjust to seeing and relying on the ceiling fans overhead.

"Mom, Manisha Maushi came in early to make *parathas* for me!" Ronak was excited to see so much planning for his breakfast. Mom's regular cook, who usually sprang into action around ten-thirty a.m., had come early just for our breakfast at nine.

I freshened up and saw the cup of tea waiting for me that Mom had lovingly prepared. I stopped by the kitchen to say hi to Manisha and handed her a small bag of American chocolates for her kids. In exchange, I took the plate of *methi parathas* with chili pickle and loads of butter she offered. Then I swung by the living room to chat with Mom over *parathas* and a cup of chai. Mom had already seated Ronak at the table with a glass of milk and a plateful of *parathas*. I relaxed in my sofa seat and breathed in the steamy ginger tea aroma before taking a sip.

Mom seemed thrilled to be chatting with her grandson as he narrated our Disney World experience with a detailed list of various animals he'd seen in the Animal Kingdom. A momentous occasion like this morning, eating breakfast with her grandchild, was not an everyday occurrence, so she gave Ronak her undivided attention.

Sitting back and observing them, I took in their excited conversation with teary eyes. I wanted to hold that moment in my memory forever. This incredible bond between grandma and grandson had existed right from Ronak's birth. Mom had visited us in America to support and guide me through my delivery. She came well prepared with various colorful baby suits, gold chains, silver anklets, a silver spoon, a silver cup, and many other goodies to welcome the arrival of my baby boy.

"Why do you insist on gold and silver, Mom? I don't get it," I had argued with her before she'd embarked, hoping to reduce the weight of her luggage.

"Don't you worry. Our grandson will drink water only out of a silver cup and spoon. So, I am bringing them." I had rarely seen her be so assertive. After the baby's arrival, she adorned Ronak with silver anklets and gold bracelets per our Hindu customs.

In the hospital, she sat with us until a cesarean section became necessary. She had always been my pillar of strength, and that day, as they rolled my bed to surgery, she courageously walked beside me and then stood beside Neeraj in support as he signed the authorization forms. When Neeraj entered the operating room, Mom waited in the waiting room all alone, without any reluctance.

After my C-section, the doctor presented Ronak, wrapped in a receiving blanket, looking like a white bunny rabbit with pink cheeks. Then they took this bundle of joy to meet his grandma, placed him in her arms, and congratulated her on becoming a grandmother. A strong, special bond was established that day. After all, she had traveled thousands of miles to a different continent for this little angel. The minute she held him in her arms, she was in seventh heaven.

"Mom, what should we do today?" Ronak's question nudged me out of my reverie.

His endless energy and enthusiasm surprised me; my own jet-lagged body was becoming more aware of the humidity. I had only extra sleep on my mind but said nothing to that effect.

Blotting the beads of sweat on my forehead, I answered, "Maybe we can go see our apartment with Grandma."

"Finish up your breakfast, take your bath, and then we can go." Mom stepped in to encourage Ronak; I didn't have to worry. Although my body felt heavy with jet lag, my mind relaxed under the cooling shade of my mother's love. I sipped on my ginger-flavored tea and put a piece of *methi paratha* in my mouth, and its ingredients—fenugreek greens, flour, garlic, ginger, cumin powder, and coriander leaves—worked their savory magic on me. Tasty food, combined with Mom's love, seemed like heavenly happiness.

An hour later, we hired an autorickshaw to visit our new apartment in a development known as Orion Elevations. Ronak was head over heels for the autorickshaws. "I call the window seat," he said before getting into the vehicle. Mom and I followed.

"Ronak, if you are sitting in the corner, hold on to the rail carefully." I was worried because the autorickshaw, like most others, had no doors and was open on both sides.

"He understands. He is not that small anymore," Mom offered.

"Thank you, Aaji." Ronak was happy that Grandma was defending him.

"Ronak, you are used to your car in America, so how do you like rickshaws?" Mom asked.

It seemed I no longer had a say in this grandma-grandson conversation.

"All four doors are closed in a car, yet I must wear a seat belt," he reasoned. "I feel restricted in the car."

"That's why I asked him to hold on to the rail," I explained. "I'm worried that if the rickshaw hits a pothole, he'll be caught off guard."

"No, I can take care of myself," Ronak argued, emboldened by his grandma's reassurance. But I kept calm and focused on his safety. Being extra-cautious was my second nature as a mother. However, I felt like I was getting sandwiched between the two generations.

The journey to my apartment was only ten minutes and included crossing two traffic lights on the main Link Road. At the first signal, we found ourselves surrounded by multiple vehicles that sat so close to us. Reflexively moving aside, I made room and had Ronak sit in the center. Looking around, he agreed without arguing. I heard many vehicles surrounding us accelerate before the traffic signal changed. I warned our driver to keep a safe speed and distance, and many other drivers honked angrily while overtaking us. On reaching the next signal, we found those same vehicles waiting at the light and honking impatiently.

"This is not even the office crowd yet," the driver said quietly, glancing at my face in the rearview mirror as I cringed at every pothole and honk. He must have read the tension on my face as "not-used-to-Mumbai."

As our rickshaw turned left, I was pleasantly surprised. This road was narrower than the main road but cleaner, divided between tall, spacious office buildings on one side and the open, airy creekside swamp on the other.

"This whole area was under the creek, wasn't it?" I could barely remember.

"They reclaimed that portion and built the office buildings here," Mom explained.

After a short distance, I noticed private buses lined up on one side of the road and multiple autorickshaws on the other, narrowing the two-lane street and allowing only one vehicle to pass on each side.

Various flowering plants and exotic palm trees embellished the road. In short, this little suburban town was now exuding the ambiance of an upscale locality. The spacious buildings flaunted a few familiar names, such as Sony Entertainment, JPMorgan Chase, and others. While in America, I had heard about many jobs being outsourced to India. Now, I was witnessing one such location where perhaps those jobs were subcontracted. The entire strip was full of BPO (business process outsourcing), telemarketing, and online supporting offices right up until we reached the residential area.

This bustling landscape reminded me of when I used to work in old Mumbai. Back in those days, whenever I visited our downtown Nariman Point office for meetings, I had to travel by rickshaw, train, and cab and face a sea of people. My destination was on the banks of the Arabian Sea, and the silhouettes of the skyscrapers on one side surrounded the semi-clean but permanently built tar roads. Once I reached my destination, a vibrant place with professionally attired people scuttling toward their workplaces, I always felt energized and happy to be contributing to India's economic capital. And now, sixteen years later, looking at this suburban office street, I experienced a similar emotional lift, even though I was not yet a member of the workforce in this part of the world.

As the rickshaw covered a short distance, we noticed that two extensive gardens were planted high on the old garbage dumping ground. The innovative creation of these gardens seemed to have made this locality competitive with Mumbai's upper-crust real estate. A variety of shrubs, vines, flowering plants, and palm trees made the garden look inviting. The creepers of bougainvillea on the tall fences were in full summer bloom, painting the entire wall pink and white. I had never seen suburban Mumbai so beautiful; it seemed like a picture out of one of Tripadvisor's destination pages.

Noticing my amazed expression, the driver supplied the name. "This is Mindspace."

"Okay, how far is Orion Elevations?"

He pointed at the three tall buildings a short distance ahead.

"That's our apartment complex, Ronak."

"An apartment in such a tall building?" Ronak whispered. He had seen skyscrapers only as our workplaces in downtown Denver. In the mountain state of Colorado, the houses in our neighborhood had two stories; the apartment buildings in the suburbs stood at three to four stories, max.

Our Visit to Our Apartment

Those tall buildings reminded me of our visit two years earlier to Orion Elevations to view the model apartment before buying.

Being a proud homeowner in America and having undergone the thrilling house-shopping experience there, on our first visit to Orion Elevations, I was very excited and prepared to be dazzled by this Mumbai model apartment. I expected it to be decked out in expensive designer upgrades and feature every possible amenity to generate interest and quick sales. So, when the builder's sales office team accompanied us to the model flat in 2007, I was disappointed to see bare walls in an empty apartment. However, I was glad for the extensive use of granite for the kitchen and bathroom countertops, the use of designer tiles for flooring, and the bathrooms showing off medicine cabinets, a rarity in old Mumbai. Giant sliding glass doors led to all the balconies, and there was excellent closet space. The ceiling was high compared with the ones elsewhere in Mumbai. The apartment features were lovely, but I had hoped to see extravagant designer details and decorations in the model home, just like in America. Still, after looking at all the alternatives, we quickly returned and booked the Orion Elevations apartment.

Ronak rushed inside the brightly lit, spacious main lobby as soon as we exited the autorickshaw. It was a vast, echoing space, standing two stories tall, with a waiting area for guests, a center wall listing all the residents' names, and security personnel scrutinizing visitors and making them sign the visitor logbook. The lobby's chic granite flooring complemented three tall elevators with shiny stainless-steel doors. Ronak loved the elevator's button display panel.

Once we exited the elevator, Mom directed us to our new home. The corridor was rectangular and spacious, with two apartments on each side of the elevators. As we unlocked the door to our unit, I realized this was our first real estate in Mumbai.

"Our apartment!" I said out loud with joy. What a feeling! It was liberating to escape the chicken-or-egg situation that had long troubled me and prevented us from taking the plunge. But now, I was ecstatic about stepping into our own Mumbai apartment for the first time. As soon as we entered, I smelled the new paint on the walls. After sliding the balcony door open, I could inhale a faint fresh aroma from that morning's rain. The apartment had prominent light-colored designer tile flooring, making the space look more extensive, while the high ceiling enhanced that effect.

My spirit lifted with joy as we completed this next step in our family adventure.

CR

9

Anxious About School

June 2009

S till settling in before classes began, I visited Ronak's Mumbai school to submit our certificates and paperwork and pay the tuition fees. I also needed the list of required books and supplies. Demanding that I come the next day, the clerk insisted that the list had been shared with students on the last day of school. The following day, after waiting for an hour, I received the list from the clerk. During my wait, I thought about C2E Charter School in Colorado. Every year, as soon as we registered for the next academic year, C2E provided us with the lists of dos and don'ts and required supplies. *But you're no longer living in the States*, I reminded myself.

The new school's requirements comprised a long checklist of books, workbooks, notebooks, a dictionary, and an atlas. The school uniform items—shoes, socks, tie, blazer—were listed with the tailor's name and address. In contrast, Ronak's school in Colorado instructed parents to buy school uniforms from Walmart or Target—any solid-colored polo shirt and khaki or navy-colored trousers were sufficient. Although the sweater had to be a specific color, the school flexibly left the store choice to the parents.

But in this Mumbai international school, kids were required to wear a blazer and tie despite the tropical weather. Most importantly, the uniform had to be bought from the tailor named on the list. With this kind of monopoly, one would think that the tailor probably cooperated with parents; however, he took every student's measurements toward the end of the academic year at the school, so parents had to take the student to the tailor's shop if the child missed school that day. I later realized that these expensive, average-quality uniforms would be delivered not at the customer's convenience but whenever the tailor decided.

"Are lockers available so students can leave their heavy books at school and just bring home the lighter ones?" I inquired after glancing at the number of books on the list.

The clerk had yet to make eye contact with me, but as soon as I finished asking my question, she tilted her head away from her screen and gawked at me. I felt more offended by that gaze than by her trying to ignore me earlier.

"Nobody gets a locker at school!" The clerk glared.

"That's okay," I reasoned. "I'll send my son with a wheeled bag so he doesn't have to carry so many books on his back." Based on our previous school experience, I knew the answers to most of the questions. Well, almost!

The clerk looked shocked. "Here, we treat books as goddesses, and we do not drag those over the floor, so you cannot send a wheeled bag with a student!"

For a moment, I faltered, not believing my ears. Don't people drag airline bags containing books and laptops? Don't college students and office workers use laptop bags with wheels? That was the new normal now. Besides, nobody was insulting Vidya (the goddess of learning and knowledge); in fact, people protected knowledge by encasing it. I thought I was enrolling my child in an international school, but this clerk seemed to be a galaxy away from the global world. First, she'd avoided me, and now, she was suddenly explaining the difference between "here" and "there" because she had Ronak's admission form that revealed we'd come from the U.S.

I am a brown-skinned woman like her, speak the local lingo, and am also educated in India. I also treat any book like a goddess. Yet, just because we moved here from America, this clerk lectures me on being respectful toward Vidya? I was disappointed and offended by her ridiculous behavior, but I held my tongue rather than risk Ronak being treated differently based on my actions.

"Don't send him there," Neeraj urged when I shared this story over the telephone.

"But this school seems good academically, and it's an ICSE school," I argued.

"But I don't understand; if they are completely oblivious to the concept of lockers or wheeled bags, then why do they even attach 'International' to their name?" He had a valid point.

I'm sure we'll adjust, I told myself. *These are simply growing pains we're certain to overcome.*

CR

10

Our Impression of a Modern Mumbai

With our American furniture shipment in transit and the Mumbai apartment awaiting interior updates, Ronak and I roosted at Mom's for two months. Neeraj still remained in America, fulfilling his existing commitments and evaluating job prospects in India. It was a challenging time, as we dearly missed our tight little family unit. Later, because both my sisters were out of Mumbai, I extended our stay at Mom's until September so Mom wouldn't be staying alone at her apartment.

Meanwhile, I relished having cooking and cleaning help available daily at Mom's. Manisha made hot, delicious food for us every day from a menu chosen by Mom. The feeling that somebody was cooking for me without my having to fret about it was very comforting. I had daydreamed about this convenience for the past thirteen years in America, so my present contentment strengthened my conviction that our decision to move was correct. I was convinced settling in India would not be as tough as some friends back in America had made it sound. My mom was always there for us whenever we needed an emotional boost or help with logistics, which greatly eased this initial transition from west to east.

Feeling settled at Mom's, I focused on hiring carpenters, interior decorators, and painters. Automatically, I searched for the options available on the internet. Disheartened after extensive searching yielded no results, I concluded that even in 2009, Indian businesses were not yet utilizing the web. Especially when it came to buying quality furniture and upholstery, people here had no faith in the power of the internet and would instead visit the shop or showroom or even rely on word of mouth. I was genuinely perplexed by this.

Eventually, I accepted the reality that no furniture store would give me a virtual peek at its stock. I would have to visit the shops in person to find basic beds and sofa sets.

My education on the present-day Mumbai continued. I knew that one could never escape the city's heat or mass of people. Being an industrial city and a unique destination, Mumbai attracted people from all over India. Accommodating these population demands resulted in a never-ending flurry of construction that included the conversion of dilapidated chawl dwellings—old tenements in dire need of repairs—into sprawling tower projects. This caused a lot of air pollution and often created a thin layer of dust over interior furniture, creating one more job, dusting, for maids in every household.

While at Mom's, I oversaw the buying of groceries. Amid the sizzling heat or seasonal rain flooding the potholes in the crowded street markets, I was glad to find an air-conditioned supermarket. It felt like an oasis during the hot, sunny days. This two-story supermarket reminded me of Walmart; I was particularly pleased to find specific food items there. Thinking we would not get them in India, I had brought a few snacks like Oreo cookies, peanut butter,

Ronak's favorite cereals, Pop-Tarts, and cereal bars from America.

The store was one of a kind, popular, and often crowded. Once we waited in a long line, we could finally enter but only after an elaborate security screening. When Ronak and I couldn't find the frozen Tater Tots, I asked a young sales associate. These new stores seemed to have attracted a young age group hailing from a humble background who were either college students or fresh graduates in a sales or stock clerk capacity. I felt a lot older when I saw them springing into action immediately upon a customer's inquiry. They were always ready to assist; but because of their aggressive promotion of products, it was often easy to end up making an unintended purchase. The sales associate promptly returned with frozen chicken *kathi kabab* rolls. "We don't have Tater Tots, but you might enjoy these, which are on discount today," she offered.

Ronak was happy to see chicken sausages, so we kept them. Immediately handpicking two more frozen products, the clerk then tried to promote those, but we managed to escape with only what we needed. Ronak was curious about not seeing buy-one-get-one-free promotions. "There is a huge population of people like us buying these products, especially foreign products," I explained. "So, when they sell out fast, stores don't have to promote them with a buy-one-get-one-free deal."

People rushed around the store wielding their carts like race cars. Having secured everything on our list, we joined the checkout line. When we stood at the end of our line, it almost reached the aisles. Maintaining a safe distance, I kept my cart away from the shopper ahead of me, but in a few minutes, other shoppers heading for the aisles started cutting and crossing our line, using the space in front of my cart. *I'm definitely not in Denver anymore*, I mused.

Besides the cook and maids at Mom's home, other service members complemented her household. A newspaper deliveryman and milkman would ring the bell around seven a.m., and a sanitation worker would collect trash later in the morning. With one phone call, we could reach fruit and vegetable vendors who would spring back and forth to deliver the order in her neighborhood.

While adjusting to the "new" Mumbai, I searched for the Mumbai where I grew up. After all the planning and decision-making that we'd done to change countries, I was here. Still, at times, contemporary Mumbai felt unrecognizable and did not quite measure up to the Mumbai in my memory. When I criticized anything and expressed my dismay, my relatives told me I shouldn't make a mountain out of a molehill. It was hard for me to recognize this new face of Mumbai; it had changed.

I also found myself unable to comprehend the disregard for cleanliness in the city. "Spotlessness" seemed like a subjective term here, a situation that had worsened in the past thirteen years. Cleanliness should start from the personal and extend to the societal level. Everyone seemed to clean their houses well, but some people didn't hesitate to throw out cigarettes, tickets, and papers on the roads. In some communities, even cut vegetables or leftover food ended up on the streets, and community cleanliness suffered.

Another significant and noticeable change after our return to Mumbai was that the area around Mom's apartment, located in a Western suburb, was booming with many outsourced companies. And the area surrounding those international businesses was beautified with meticulous landscaping and open spaces. The city boasted a financial capital's fast pace, the Bollywood buzz, and a streak of freedom and independence. I also noticed that contemporary India was young and that the Indian workforce was more youthful.

On the way to our apartment from Mom's, there were several multinational call centers. I was sure that inside those buildings, office cleanliness must have been observed, as the buildings' shiny exteriors were meticulously maintained. Outside, however, there were no trash cans in sight, so even if someone wanted to discard something into a proper container, they couldn't. Similarly, opposite these buildings, street vendors sold snacks to the personnel working day and night in those offices, and these hawkers never kept any trash cans. I found myself staring at the crowd in disbelief one hot afternoon when office workers crowded these stalls and, without thinking twice, tossed their empty beverage cups or paper plates on the ground. They certainly could never have gotten away with this behavior inside their office buildings. Perhaps they were too hungry to be bothered by the unclean roads or the traffic congestion caused by the hawkers' carts. And yet, if the hawkers had made the *vada* chutney less spicy, their customers would have complained; that's how picky we Indians are as food connoisseurs.

Unfortunately, those professionals seemed to escape social account-ability and ownership of their actions, even when they threw cigarette butts on the road before heading back inside the office buildings. While the hawkers didn't think about their surroundings, I expected the office workers to have been more aware and to have urged the vendors to make arrangements so the trash piling up around their stalls would be cleaned up. If the customers had banded together to effect change, the sellers would have had to comply; but I never witnessed those individuals going that extra mile.

This was the opposite of what we'd experienced in Colorado, where people were mindful of trash and automatically threw out any waste in a trash can, at least in the upper-middle-class areas. With everyone following the rules, the system functioned like a well-oiled machine.

Both India and the U.S. are democratic societies, and my grandfather would have agreed that democracy requires each citizen to do their bit for the common good.

I'm aware that we were looking at the same issue from two different lenses—I from my time already spent in America, and they from their life in India, I had been away from for so many years. In the end, we were all Indians, and I knew I had to open my heart to the new India.

ℭℜ

11

The First Month of School Was Quite an Experience!

On the first day of school, as I was taking Ronak there, he was quiet, and my heart sank when I looked at his face—so anxious. He had already experienced the first days of the first four grades in the U.S., but this was the first day of fifth grade, and not just in a different school, but in a different city, country, and continent altogether. I held his hand in mine for some time. "I will be waiting at the school gate all day long," I assured him while gently squeezing his hand. "Don't think for a minute that Mom will go home; I will be right outside the school building if you need me, Ronak." Ronak stood still, gazing up at me with his apprehensive face. "*Beta*, if you need me, you just let the teachers know that you want to see your mom, and I will come and get you." As soon as I said this, he eased up a bit. "Now, let's see that smile," I cajoled him. Ronak tried to obscure his doubt and concern behind a vague smile.

Once we entered the building, the help desk personnel informed us that the fifth-grade classroom was on the second floor. As we started climbing the poorly lit staircase, I thought, *I can't wait for the school's move to the new building*.

On the second floor, the teachers in the corridor said they would take care of the children and that parents need not worry. One teacher, familiar with most of the kids, looked at Ronak and instantly recognized a new student. With a kind smile, she assured me, "I will take him to his class." She seemed like an angel, gently guiding my son to his new classroom. In contrast to their office staff, she seemed very warm.

Once the kids were settled in their respective classes, she returned to instruct all the anxious parents waiting in the corridor to leave the school building, so classes could begin. She urged me not to worry and suggested I could quickly check on my son. So, before heading out to the gate, I peeked into Ronak's classroom and saw him sitting silently at his desk. He seemed to just be gazing at his writing desk; but as a mother, I could tell that, although he appeared composed, underneath, he was a little shaken up. At this point, I could vouch for how well he managed himself, considering his new surroundings, because I was admittedly feeling lost in that new location too. I waved and reminded him by miming that I was not going anywhere and that I would be available right outside school if he needed me. With a blank gaze, Ronak looked away and focused on the teacher sitting in front of the classroom.

As I exited the school building, I felt my stomach churning with stress. A few other parents waited at the gate. After exchanging hellos, I realized most were first or second-grade students' parents. While telling them about Ronak, I didn't care how they must have viewed me, worried sick about a fifth grader. At that moment, the only thing that mattered was my son and his ease of transition into this new world.

As the other parents began to leave, I realized that even though I'd promised to stay there all day long, it was impractical. So, I returned to the school office to ask if I could wait there. I was fortunate to see the teacher who had led Ronak to his classroom a few minutes earlier. Thanking her for her help, I introduced myself and explained that Ronak was making a start in a new country and school. Then I learned that the teacher, Mrs. Shivpure, was the vice principal of the school. She encouraged me to leave my number with her and assured me she would call me personally if Ronak needed help that day. With her assurance, I felt comfortable about finally going home.

When I returned to pick up Ronak in the afternoon, I stood outside the gate along with several other parents eagerly waiting to see their kids. After the bell rang, many students began running down the staircase, even though some teachers and senior students warned everyone against running. After almost half of the students had come down, I saw Ronak descend from the second floor. My heart was beating fast out of concern and curiosity. Once he spotted me in the crowd of parents, he smiled and waved, his face now at ease. The minute I saw his relaxed appearance, I could no longer contain my emotions. I gave in to tears, releasing the anxiety and guilt of putting my son through this experience.

Ronak ran and hugged me, but before I could ask how school was, we were interrupted by a very tall boy from Ronak's class, reminding Ronak to bring a particular book to class the next day.

Finally, after ten minutes of pleading with several autorickshaw drivers in that sea of people, we located one who happily transported us to Mom's home.

"How was your day?" Grandma asked, concealing her worries with a smile.

"Okay," Ronak answered, distracted by the TV in the living room. "This school is different, Mom," he said once he settled in.

"Different? How?" I asked.

"Everyone talks so differently; teachers even instructed us not to use Hindi in school. They suggested using only English to communicate with other students. But the minute the teachers left the classroom, everyone switched to Hindi."

"Did you speak to them in Hindi?"

"Why should I when they told us not to?"

"Oh, such an obedient child!" Grandma said as I just nodded.

But then Ronak opened up, saying, "Mom, you gave me the wrong books for school."

"What? Wrong books?" I cringed. I already carried a burden in my mind for bringing my child to a new country and new school. Now, it looked as if I hadn't even accomplished the simple task of procuring the right books for him. However involuntarily, I had jeopardized his universe. I was embarrassed.

"Yes, wrong books! Everyone had brown books, and I don't have any brown books," he explained.

Okay, whoosh! I intuitively understood from my own childhood experience in the Indian school system, and, feeling exonerated, I smiled.

"Well, Ronak, I'm sure your classmates' books were the same as the ones we bought, but their parents have probably spent a fair amount of time before the first day of school neatly covering their books in brown paper."

"But why would anyone cover the books? How do they tell the books apart if they're covered?" Hailing from the American school system, Ronak failed to understand.

"My dear son, it is a little different on this side of the globe," I explained. "First, in schools here, book covers count toward tidiness. Second, people are more vigilant here about preservation and economizing; they would hate for the book to be torn and to be replaced in the same academic year."

"And they might want to pass on the same book to a younger sibling, so spoiling it is not an option for many," Grandma quickly added.

"How boring is that! I love the detailed pictures they have printed on our geography and history books. I don't want those pictures covered," Ronak enlightened us, leaving Mom and me laughing.

I couldn't help but continue to smile and quickly analyze that stark difference in my mind. When my teachers had instructed me to use book covers in my school days, I had followed the instructions blindly. But Ronak's objection was logical; how would you differentiate one book from another at a glance? I remembered that I used to have an early morning school schedule in my fifth grade. Not being a morning person, I barely made it for the school's first bell on time. Looking back, if I'd been able to tell my books apart with only one glance while packing my school bag, it would have saved me from many "LATE" marks at school. But I had never asked why. I was proud of my son for having his own perspective and not just following the herd.

Later that evening, when Neeraj phoned, Ronak was fast asleep, which gave me a better opportunity to share stories from the first day of school. Neeraj chuckled when he heard the brown paper story.

I said, "I remember my school was not that particular about

book covers, yet my parents always covered the books with newspaper. The notebooks for essay writing had to be strictly covered in brown paper."

"Even our school was not that particular about brown paper," Neeraj reminisced.

Over the following weeks, Ronak did his best to adjust to the new school environment. One area that seemed harder to adjust to was the language. "Every time the teacher walks out of the classroom, everyone switches to Hindi," Ronak told me again one day. This was something I hadn't expected to hear after enrolling Ronak in an English medium school. Still, in this school, apparently, most of the kids were far more comfortable communicating in Hindi than in English. However, Ronak had grown up hearing Hindi, either in old Bollywood films his dad obsessed over or at the occasional *desi* gatherings in Colorado. Although I had been teaching him the basics of Hindi reading and writing for a couple of months now, he had never really been in a situation where he'd need to speak it. And now, he was in a classroom where kids bantered effortlessly in loose informal Mumbai Hindi, and he was exposed to all sorts of words, phrases and bad words he had never heard before.

One day, Ronak came home and remarked that kids in his class spoke English and Hindi differently. One girl named Karuna was asked in class, "Who hibernates during winter?" Karuna had replied, "Beer."

"How can they mess up a simple word like 'bear,' Mom?" Being a wildlife lover, Ronak was baffled.

Really, I can't believe it either; this is an English medium school! I vented silently.

But I had to give Ronak a logical explanation. "Well, most of these kids are new to English, and they usually stick to their mother tongue at home, so lack of practice in English conversation does bring out these mistakes, Ronak."

He gave that scenario careful thought, just like on other occasions when he was subjected to similar speculations over his Hindi.

"Aai, you never taught me the Hindi my classmates speak."

"Why do you say that? Maybe you didn't understand a few words here and there?"

"Do you know that all the boys commonly use the word *abbe* in my class?" Ronak looked at me curiously.

I couldn't grasp why boys Ronak's age were using Hindi slang words in the classroom. I made a mental note to talk to the teachers about this. In the meantime, I warned my son, "Don't worry! It is slang, and they should not use it in school, so you stay away from such words."

During that time, while some of Ronak's classmates enrolled in extra coaching classes, I tutored Ronak in Hindi and Marathi at home. Although the Devanagari script is similar, these languages are grammatically different. It was challenging for him, but many years of watching some parts of Hindi movies and speaking Marathi at home probably came to his rescue during the first year. Yet, when it was time for his first test, I explained anxiously to his Hindi teacher that he was studying Hindi at the first-grade level while his class was studying the language at the third-grade level. So, I formally requested that Ronak have the Hindi test at the first-grade level, and she kindly agreed. Come midterm, I asked for the same, but seeing Ronak's progress in the classroom, she convinced me, "If your child wants to run, you should not force him to walk one step at a time. Let him run. He is ready." I was so grateful to her for that lesson and her assurance.

Soon, Ronak caught up with the class in Hindi and progressed effortlessly. At the end of his first year, I asked him how he felt about the Indian school and how he had adjusted.

Without delay, he answered, "It's okay. But I feel there is never a dull moment in the classroom."

For Ronak, India offered a slice of heaven—a deep bond with his grandma. He would stay at grandma's place almost once a month while in fifth, sixth, and seventh grades. He was an only child in Neeraj's and my immediate family, so we didn't mind it either. Grandma's home was a very welcoming addition to Ronak's life, and his presence was great for my mom as well.

Even though many questions remained, seeing my son so happy, thriving in school, and enjoying our new life helped ease my earlier concerns.

12

A Rainy Afternoon in Mumbai

We had booked our Mumbai apartment from one of India's supposed A-list construction companies. However, despite the tall painted walls, tall glass enclosures on all the balconies, and utility sections, the apartment was not equipped with any kitchen cabinets, closet shelves, or closet doors. The balconies had railings about three feet high, and being on the fifth floor, I worried that the short barrier posed a safety hazard since Ronak was still at an age where he might run around the house bouncing a soccer ball. So, I approached a few contractors about the job of installing a higher barrier and kitchen cabinets.

One afternoon in July, I was meeting one such contractor at the apartment. It had rained in the morning, and the sun was tilting toward the west when I reached the apartment. The weather was playing tricks, with clouds covering the sun one moment and clearing up the next. Suddenly, I heard a roar of thunder, and it began drizzling. I inhaled the fresh, earthy fragrance. Soon, rain poured from the sky. Excited, I went out to peer down from our balcony, happily observing the rain for some time and gauging its impact. I could see big, beautiful raindrops turning into small, shallow streams on the ground and flowing around the walls of the building and the parking structure. Soon, with the heavy rain showers, the huge garden lawn on top of the parking structure was submerged underwater, making the staircase to the garden look like a waterfall, bringing all that garden water to the ground.

The sound of water rushing through the pipes that ran from the terrace to the ground on the building's side wall also competed for my attention. But all these stimuli were astonishingly soothing. I was experiencing the Indian monsoon rain after a long, long time. For the past thirteen years in Denver, I had missed this dazzling rain. Although Colorado's white snow mesmerized me, in my mind, it always lacked the roaring monsoon action.

It was now close to three p.m., and the contractor was nowhere to be seen, so I decided to sit on the lonely floor mat in an empty bedroom. The rain showers had disappeared after an hour, allowing the sun to peek out of the clouds. I went to the balcony again; the temperature seemed to have dropped, leaving the gentle, cool breeze to wave over me. As I ran my fingers through my hair, my eyes met a vast, open area outside our complex, beyond the manicured garden. The monsoon had blessed that area with small bushes, and flowering weeds sprouted in all directions. The space also had a patch of lush green grass almost two feet tall. This entire section of wildflowers and grass blades swayed to the tune of the monsoon wind. Seeing this beautiful ballet under the cloudy sky with the cool breeze stroking my face and hair felt magical and spellbinding.

It reminded me of my childhood monsoon memories of times when we played with joy and laughter and without inhibition amid those tall green grasses filled with wildflowers. And suddenly, realizing something deep, I smiled, delighted with the feeling that *I was home.*

CR

PART THREE

Fun and Not-So-Fun Experiences

13

Happy! Neeraj Is Home

While Ronak and I got acquainted with the new school in India, Neeraj continued working in Denver, far from his family. He sorely missed seeing Ronak and his new universe. One evening in July, as I tucked Ronak into bed, Neeraj phoned and we talked for an hour over his lunch break, which was at one a.m. for me in India. Neeraj shared great news—he had convinced his current client to let him work from India for the remaining three months of his project, which meant he could join us in Mumbai in the next month. We mutually decided to rely on our savings after his project finished until we lined up job opportunities in India.

Around the end of August 2009, Neeraj joined us in India, and we were thrilled to be reunited as a family. Ronak had missed his father dearly for the past three months.

Soon after, our container shipment from America also arrived. That consignment of fifty-six huge boxes carrying our belongings from America ignited the need to move to our apartment. This shipment completely submerged most of the living room and a large bedroom in our Orion Elevations apartment. While still housed at my mom's, we dutifully dropped Ronak at school and visited our apartment daily to unpack boxes.

We decided to move in on the auspicious day of Dussehra, a Hindu festival that celebrates the victory of good over evil. So, I thought, *What better day to justify our new beginning, our sincere efforts to replant ourselves, and be truthful to our roots?* We were very enthusiastic about this move. At the same time, I was a little anxious, as the actual experience of living independently as a family in India would now commence once we concluded our stay at my mom's well-managed abode.

United at last! For the past three months, making decisions for Ronak, myself, and our new apartment every day, and visiting stores and bureaucratic offices to buy furniture or arrange for a cooking gas connection or set up a cable connection had been exhausting for me. Finally, Neeraj and I could share those responsibilities and brainstorm solutions to other questions facing us in the new country.

Once in our apartment, I stuck my Hem's List on the refrigerator; I needed to focus on the essential bullet points:

- Household help
- Driver *(okay, a tiny detail seems missing—we had to buy a car first)*
- Custom furniture *(on the way)*
- Colorful walls *(before the festival)*

From our balcony, we watched the whole building complex come alive every evening with the giggles of kids playing in the manicured garden on top of the parking structure. Younger kids enjoyed the see-saw, swings, and slides placed in a sandbox, while a few older kids played soccer after dark, around seven p.m. We learned later that most of the older kids attended their extra coaching classes after school; that's why they played later, after sunset, once they returned home.

"Why are they playing soccer in the concrete parking lot?" Ronak wondered one evening. "They will get hurt."

I remembered reading in the newspaper just a month earlier that this island city had a disproportionately small ratio of playgrounds to population.

City authorities would rent out a few playgrounds for weddings during the wedding season. On other occasions, if any religious guru visited the city, they held religious gatherings on the playgrounds for four to five days. I recalled that the open spaces surrounding my mom's building were always rented out, and it was a massive issue for her community during the wedding seasons to keep the noise levels down and the roads clear. But I chose not to unload all these details on Ronak's sensitive mind.

"It seems in the absence of a playground in our complex, kids have no choice but to play in the parking lot," I said.

"That's weird." Ronak grimaced.

But that was the reality of this forever-growing city, I guess.

Going Out for a Stroll

After we settled into our apartment, Neeraj suggested sometime in October, "We should start our routine and get fresh air, especially now that the rains have stopped completely."

I couldn't agree more. So, one evening, we put on our comfortable clothing and workout shoes and decided to walk. We also managed to get Ronak to put on his bicycle gear: helmet, tennis shoes, elbow pads, and knee pads. He carried his favorite brand-new

RipStik that Neeraj had brought from America. Even though he detested wearing the helmet and knee pads, Ronak knew I wouldn't allow casterboarding without his safety gear, so he didn't argue.

Finally, all prepared, we arrived at the elevated rectangular garden above the huge parking garage. Landscaped with various tropical plants and flowers, the garden was located opposite our building, which was one of three that lined two adjacent sides of the park. There were two staircases and one long, elevated ramp leading up to the garden. We chose the ramp, hoping to get more steps on my pedometer. Making our way through the *chapha* flower bushes, we arrived at this lush green park. Ronak couldn't stop admiring it and wondered how they managed to prevent water from seeping into the parking lot underneath.

We smiled and explained as we walked on the broad, tiled pathway that resembled a python and encircled two circular structures sitting at both ends of the park. One round frame filled with sand hosted the slides and swings, and the other was armored with a concrete floor surrounded by benches. The fresh air energized us after our busy indoor house projects.

"Finally, our family time together!" Ronak smiled and held our hands. We realized it was our first-ever legitimate outdoor family time with Neeraj since moving to India.

Soon, Ronak jumped on his RipStik and rode around the hard-surfaced circle. Staying out of his way, we sat on one of the concrete benches around the circle, hoping to chat with each other. Ronak spoke to us whenever he came near our bench.

For some reason, I noticed a large group of women sitting at the other end of the park. I sensed they were whispering among themselves and were looking in our direction. But I brushed off the thought as Ronak swung around on the RipStik and called out for our attention.

Upon arriving in India five months earlier, desperate to make Ronak's stay more exciting, I looked everywhere for this new caster-board called RipStik. But all the shops in Mumbai showed me a picture of a skateboard instead and said if we insisted on the casterboard, they could order it from America. I immediately knew I had to ask Neeraj to buy the casterboard in the U.S. and bring it with him. Ronak's eyes widened in astonishment when he saw the RipStik in Neeraj's luggage. He jumped for joy when he saw his dad after three months and also his new prized possession. Since that day, Ronak had diligently practiced on his brand-new ride in the apartment and our corridor.

"Ronak, I am so impressed with your progress." As I waved at him, I caught a glimpse of the same group of women eyeing my family.

"Baba, why don't you try to ride it?" Ronak called to Neeraj.

Neeraj joined him and learned the tips he so freely offered. In Neeraj's efforts to understand the technique, he gyrated in place, and Ronak began laughing loudly. I was happy to hear his laughter. It was rare to come by in those days after our move. I quickly dried my tears.

It took about ten to fifteen minutes for Neeraj to master it, and then he gave it a try without losing his balance once. As we cheered and applauded his efforts, Neeraj's grin widened. Ronak pulled him away for yet another round. As the father-son duo moved forward, my focus shifted to the surrounding people and landed again on that cluster of women sitting in the other corner of the park, still focused on us. Among them, I noticed a few acquaintances I had made over the past three months while walking in and out of our building. So, I waved at them from where I sat, and they immediately waved back. That confirmed they had been observing us. Feeling both vulnerable and annoyed, I nonchalantly looked away.

After his gallant ride on the RipStik, Neeraj returned to share his new experience with me while Ronak resumed riding. As we sat, I continued noticing other people nearby. The park was crowded compared to my neighborhood park in Denver. Nevertheless, being surrounded by so many people felt great. I saw many kids playing in the garden; the adults who were present mostly mingled with others of their age group, just like those women gossiping. Senior citizens were either sitting or walking gingerly with their peers. Men walked with other men, while older women strolled separately with their women friends. Surprisingly, with the exception of one or two new mothers, no parents accompanied their kids. With help readily available, the younger kids were with nannies.

"Did you notice, among the people around, no one is in the park with their family?" I pointed out, perplexed. With this realization, I told Neeraj, "Maybe that's why those women were staring—we are the only family spending time together in the garden!"

"Think about it," Neeraj said. "Working parents have longer commutes in a city like Mumbai; probably not everyone gets to spend evening time with their family."

"Maybe they were admiring our happiness?"

"I sure would like to believe so."

With his wide-eyed smile, Ronak called, "Look, I am circling nonstop!" We watched him with sheer joy; he was getting the hang of it and completed two nonstop RipStik rounds.

Soon, it grew dark, and the chirping birds flew away as the sunlight faded, leaving a few shades of red-orange-gray on the horizon. As I sat looking at the light fading behind the buildings around me, I also thought of the sunlight shining on the Colorado mountains, where the sun, at that moment, was just about to rise.

CR

14

Carpenter's Rule Book

Before the move, I had hoped that instead of buying Chinese-made or IKEA-style assemble-it-yourself furniture, we would design our own interior furnishings and have them customized by skilled Indian carpenters. At a minimum, we needed a wardrobe and a bed before we could settle into our apartment. On my previous visit to India, I had noticed a street near my apartment booming with several furniture showrooms, some single-story, while others, two-story, but all bustling with business. Although not as big as IKEA or an American furniture store, they typically had a few types of wardrobes, bed sets, sofa sets, and center tables on display. A hefty collection of design books, illustrated with photos of additional furniture, complemented the sample pieces. These stores tempted potential customers with enticing promises along the lines of, "We custom-make your dream furniture and deliver it to your doorstep."

Short-listing one such showroom, I placed an order for the bedroom set. They promised to manufacture the furniture in their factory, deliver it, and also install it in our apartment. I loved this idea of no mess, no clutter, and no furniture-making chaos at home.

After charging a 20 percent deposit, they guaranteed delivery in four to six weeks. But they didn't keep their promise. Even with our persistent follow-ups, they delivered after two months, one night around eight p.m. The store carpenters accompanied the delivery for installation. When I refused to let them work inside the apartment at eight p.m., they said the installation was not extensive. But by the time they had assembled and placed the furniture, it was eleven-thirty p.m., and since it was so late, they left in a hurry, leaving plywood pieces and some fallen nails on the floor, tucked away behind the door. *So much for the idea of no mess, no noise*, I thought. Thankfully, our building was fairly new, with no neighbors on our floor or the floor below us, so I guess the noise went unnoticed. Nevertheless, for the next batch of furniture, we opted to hire a carpenter instead of ordering from a giant showroom where the salesperson remains unavailable after the sale, and there's no one to contact if there's a problem with delivery or installation.

Once we moved to our apartment, the need for storage started teasing us every day. We had our ideas of this perfect handyman-cum-carpenter, but he had yet to appear, so we kept looking. We briefly considered hiring an interior decorator but quickly realized that wouldn't work; a decorator is only worth the expense if you have a complete apartment makeover in mind. You also have to surrender your house keys to them. We couldn't do that because our apartment was both our living space and a makeshift workplace during office hours. Besides, we weren't ready to invest in a makeover of our brand-new apartment when we were not even sure we would stay that long in India.

So, I compromised and decided on a house makeover in phases, designing the furniture according to my vision. One day, during his second visit, I told Pande, carpenter number 1, "The room door should split two ways to give way to the bookcase behind the door."

"But you should not keep the furniture behind the door," Pande said, failing to understand the requirement.

"That's how I want the door."

"It won't look good," he warned.

"Yes, but we do not have that luxury here in Mumbai's real estate."

"True, but you can get the bookcase pushed into the wall, and the room will also look bigger," he answered flippantly, peering behind the door. Slurping his coffee while eyeing the plate of biscuits, Pande undoubtedly had plans to extract more business from us—*making the room look bigger and all.*

"How would you make the room look bigger?" I asked curiously, offering him the plate of biscuits he'd been coveting.

"Madam, break the wall. Space will be automatically bigger," he answered, mouth stuffed with crumbs.

First of all, who breaks a wall like this? While at my parents', we had never witnessed anything like this in an apartment building. I was stunned when I tried to imagine his vision. We were on the fifth floor of a twenty-story building; breaking a wall as he suggested might threaten the columns and thus the whole building's stability and structure. "But that will weaken the building," I shrieked.

"In this building, I have done a similar job a few times." He shrugged. "People even move the door if it gets in the way and put it on some other wall," he continued, unaffected by my concern.

"Who in their right mind would do this? Does the management even permit this?" I was perplexed by his daring remarks.

"Madam, you simply don't tell them and just get the work done.

This is a new building, so it's okay." Now, he was skirting dangerously close to uncharted water, something we always avoided.

Well, I should just hire another carpenter without telling you, I retorted, but only in my mind. Rather than pursue his dangerous plan, I secured another referral from a new acquaintance in the building complex.

The new carpenter, Rajweer, a dark, middle-aged, bald man with a mouth perpetually stained red from eating *paan*, arrived after two days. Wearing a checkered shirt, neatly ironed denim trousers, and black leather shoes, he seemed utterly different from his counterparts we had seen so far. When we requested pictures of his prior work, he invited us to see his work at Kandivali.

We decided to go but were puzzled when Rajweer sent us the address, which was on the seventeenth floor. His workshop could not have been on the seventeenth floor of any building, especially in Lokhandwala Complex. He later told us it was his client's house; surprisingly, the client and his family were home when we arrived. It felt awkward to invade strangers' privacy by wandering into their house and looking at their furniture, accompanied by Rajweer's running commentary. His client's family was patient and friendly and did not seem to mind the intrusion. The family of three had just planted themselves on the sofa in front of the TV. As we moved into the kitchen, Rajweer opened a drawer to show the work he had completed, and I gasped when I saw cockroaches crawling on the cutlery.

"What?! Roaches?!"

"Oh, yes. They need to get the pest control service in here," Rajweer answered nonchalantly.

I had always known that there was a chance of this coexistence between humans and bugs in Mumbai's humid weather, but I had never in my life seen cockroaches crawling so freely and in such significant numbers in broad daylight. Although the family was welcoming and sweet, they seemed awfully sluggish to me. My mom always had a pest control service scheduled once a year, and that was enough to keep these insects at bay.

After the cockroach experience, we didn't hire carpenter number 2.

Before we could look for another, there was an urgent need to address the pigeon invasion. Regularly perched on our balcony floors, railings, and satellite TV dish, pigeons had begun spoiling the balconies with droppings everywhere. So, when we called a handyman assigned to our building, he suggested installing a fish-net over the galleries' exteriors to protect them from this invasion. Given our urgent requirement, he diligently measured the area of all four spaces and quoted Rs 10,000, which amounted to $200 at the time. Still, we never negotiated with him, as he assured us that he would use the branded-quality mesh and stainless-steel fixtures. However, on his start day, he showed up late in the evening, only to request money in advance to buy the necessary materials.

"You were supposed to start the work today, correct?" I confirmed.

"Madam, tell Sir that I need money for the material."

"That's okay. Tell me how much you need in advance so I can give it to you."

He seemed a little uncomfortable telling me the figure, and he even hesitated to accept the payment from my hand.

He returned to the building security desk at ten p.m. and informed me over the intercom that he wanted to store the materials at our place. I refused him access to the apartment so late and told him to bring the supplies back the following day because Neeraj was away for work. *How can he even ask to store the material here so late at night?* That question bothered me the most. I got my answer the following day when carpenter number 3 knocked on the door and, after depositing his tool bag on the balcony, said he was going to the twentieth floor to retrieve the mesh and fixtures.

"But why did you keep the materials upstairs? Did you keep them on the terrace?"

"Madam, I take the Central Railway to Ambernath; with the trains so crowded and our houses so small, I couldn't think of any other place. I approached my last client from the top floor, who had referred your name. Since they knew you well, they did not refuse."

Now, it made sense: When I had denied him entry to the house, carpenter number 3 had used my name to gain favor from my neighbor on the twentieth floor. I was embarrassed that he'd bothered that family. Carpenter number 3 was quite resourceful. He ended up completing the installation in four days by showing up in the second half of each day. However, two to four p.m. was the no-noise time period when drilling was off-limits. He never liked us questioning him for coming during no-noise work hours and would loudly offer some comments-cum-explanations, so we decided to part ways after he completed the task at hand. As it turned out, two years later, we found that the branded net and stainless-steel fixtures no longer prevented the pigeon invasion, forcing us to look for a new contractor. Our search for the perfect carpenter seemed never-ending.

While on my daily walk, I spoke with an acquaintance who highly recommended a carpenter named Sarvesh Gupta, who she said came from a long lineage of carpenters. "This person is sincere and always completes his work," she added.

This comment troubled me. Did it mean some carpenters here left the work half-done? Not knowing what to expect, I decided to give him a call and ask when we could meet.

"*Jee*, next Monday at ten a.m.," he replied.

By now, Neeraj had wrapped up his second work project in the U.S. and was back home with us. We wanted to design furniture mainly for our living room, as our newly delivered Italian recliners seemed lonely without an entertainment center, bookcase, and center table. So, Neeraj suggested we test the carpenter with a small task before entrusting the long list of furniture jobs to him. We had learned our lesson from the previous furniture order: Don't believe their initial boasts about their experience; instead, evaluate their delivery standards and work ethics.

"Neeraj, what do you have in mind for a small job?" I was curious.

"The spare TV we shipped from the U.S. is still in the box; it needs to be mounted on Ronak's room wall."

"But in India, wall mounting a TV is not a carpenter's job," I objected, scowling. "Why are you messing up the future contract with the carpenter before even hiring him?"

"Let's see how he handles this task," Neeraj said. "Or he may suggest another technician for this job. Besides, we don't even know where to find this kind of handyman."

I shrugged.

One hour after our appointment time and with no sign of Sarvesh, restlessly I phoned to see where he was.

"*Jee*, I'm in the building complex, sort of stuck with work."

"But we had a ten a.m. appointment," I reminded him.

"Yes, I can stop by later today."

Of course, he didn't apologize when he finally arrived at noon. However, he explained that "Mrs. Lalita" had wanted him for some work the previous week. So, before coming to us, he had completed some long-pending door work for Lalita, as she wanted him to come before her husband left for work. This carpenter number 4, Sarvesh, was a tall, middle-aged person dressed in a simple, untucked synthetic shirt and trousers. Despite his complete disregard for punctuality, he seemed very polite and down-to-earth.

When Neeraj explained the work, Sarvesh listened carefully and studied the pictures in the instruction manual with Neeraj. Without any excuses, he mounted the TV to our satisfaction the same day within two hours. During our conversation, he seemed honest with an excellent work ethic. Neeraj and I decided that he was our carpenter. We ended up not only hiring him for the living room furniture but digging deep into our pockets, we also hired him for Ronak's wardrobe and study table.

Sarvesh nodded when we shared our expectations that the work should begin at ten a.m. and wrap up before six p.m. However, for the next five days, he and his team didn't arrive until noon. So, on the sixth day, I intervened and asked him to ensure that their work began at ten.

"My assistants come from Virar. It's difficult for them to get here this early," he explained.

"But there are trains available that early," I offered helpfully.

"Madam, they cook and eat their brunch before leaving their houses, so they can't arrive by ten a.m."

Feeling exasperated, I offered no response.

Sarvesh's team made furniture in phases and began with Ronak's room. So, they had complete control over that room and even used it for a relaxing nap during the afternoon's no-noise time period.

One day, I had an epiphany regarding my ideal entertainment center, and Ronak did too, pertaining to his study table. So, I made a drawing of the table, and as soon as Sarvesh arrived, I attempted to explain it. To my dismay, I sensed cold-shouldering from him.

"Listen to me. This cupboard needs to have a foldable flap that turns into a table," I emphasized.

"Foldable table?" He shrugged.

"Yes, the table has to be collapsible."

"That won't look good," he politely dismissed.

"The flap needs to stop at two positions, so Ronak can easily work on his drawings," I continued, explaining Ronak's idea.

"Two positions? It won't be a strong table." Sarvesh scowled. "That's not even possible."

"But that's the whole point of having custom-made furniture," I argued.

"That's possible with Malaysian or Chinese furniture." Surprisingly, he suggested this was only possible in readymade furniture, without even thinking that somebody had to make that furniture too.

In the meantime, Neeraj came home from his morning run and, listening to Sarvesh's tone, decided to join our conversation.

"We need that foldable table with two positions for Ronak," Neeraj stressed. "Sir, we will try. You show us the design." Perhaps not surprisingly, Sarvesh seemed more receptive to the stern male command.

"We will go with these designs." I wasted no time in putting my design on the table and being more assertive. Sarvesh seemed less hesitant to accept the paper in the presence of male authority.

Throughout my career, I never had trouble conveying my ideas to my superiors or colleagues, most of whom had been men. Still, in this scenario, Sarvesh appeared to perceive me as subordinate to the male command. Although it felt strange, I was not surprised, as I knew some people still considered gender equality a taboo.

Lesson learned: In general, some laborers treat women differently, but I had to be firm with them and highlight my authority.

Sarvesh and his team had been working on our furniture for three consecutive months when we added a new safety door—an additional door for extra security—to the list. I had previously researched safety doors in interior decoration magazines. I had one particular maple finish in mind that was not too flashy, still classy. So, once I chose it, I sent similar images to Sarvesh. Yet one day, when I asked how soon the door would be ready, he casually replied, "Show me the pictures again."

"You still haven't made the door?" I felt silly asking this fundamental question.

"It's ready in my factory, but we must cover the surface with SunMica."

"What's SunMica?" By now, Ronak, sitting on the sofa, became interested in this new word.

"It's vinyl that covers the plywood on furniture to give a wood-like appearance. In India, they call it SunMica," I blurted out, proud of the research I had done so far.

Carefully looking at the pictures this time, Sarvesh now claimed it was a veneer, not SunMica.

"What's a veneer?" Neeraj asked the question this time.

"A thin layer of wood glued over the plywood that displays the natural beauty of wood!" Sarvesh explained.

"Is it cheaper?" Neeraj posed an obvious question.

"No, it's more expensive."

The next day, Sarvesh led us to a shop to buy the veneer sheets on priority. We chose the most natural-looking option and finalized an order for four long veneer sheets for our safety door and the surrounding walls. But Neeraj and I frowned when we heard that those sheets would cost Rs 150,000. We looked at the dream door picture and the $3,000 veneer sheets and asked Sarvesh again whether what he was proposing would resemble our dream door in the picture.

Sarvesh mumbled, "Yes, certainly."

A safety door is the face of your house, and you want it presentable, so we didn't hesitate to pay that exorbitant amount for our dream door.

We eagerly waited to see our dream door the day they brought it from Sarvesh's factory. By afternoon, we couldn't contain our excitement and asked if we could come outside to see the door. Sarvesh's team stalled for twenty minutes as they applied the finishing touches while we imagined the door and its surrounding walls outside our apartment looking fabulous in a warm maple finish.

We stepped out, excitement beaming on our faces. The next minute, our faces turned red, as the look of maple we'd been promised was nowhere in sight. Instead, we saw a very dull, yellow-looking veneer surface. Instead of brightening the entrance, it created a worn-out look.

"But you said it would look like the one in the picture." I tried to be as calm as possible.

"It's a little lighter look," Sarvesh casually acknowledged.

"But why does it look so weathered?" I challenged.

"Madam, light-dark happens," Sarvesh responded reflexively. "*Unnis-bees to hota hai*! After all, it's not a machine job!"

I couldn't believe my ears. After we had shown him the pictures, confirmed it with him ten times, even purchased the veneer with his consent, and spent Rs 150,000 just on raw material for my dream door, Sarvesh was now telling me that the results would vary. He said if you get nineteen when you look for twenty, you should not complain. A slight mistake here and there is okay. I knew, since the product was handmade, some variation would be expected, but my point was that the maple finish should not look like oak!

He'd also explained that the door was not machine-made. That was precisely the reason I'd hired him in the first place to follow my Dream Project List—Custom-Made Furniture.

This experience certainly raised the question, why did we hire a carpenter? I could very well have bought Chinese or Malaysian-made furniture and possibly a ready-made safety door and finished the whole assembly in five to six days instead of wasting energy, time, funds, and five to six months of sanity in the process.

In the end, we compromised on one point: Sarvesh used furniture stain on the safety door to brighten the dull look and make it more presentable.

Lessons learned:

1. No matter what you communicate, ensure that the communication is received and understood on the other end. Don't take the carpenter's nod as a receipt of the communication.

2. If the carpenter does not deliver what you asked for, he will always sugarcoat it by saying, "*Unnis-bees to hota hai.*" That's his motto.

☞

15

Don't Ever Test Management Principles on Your Maid!

The many joys of finally settling into our own apartment included having our own kitchen, sleeping in our own beds, making our own rules for our young son's benefit, and being able to decorate the apartment with Ronak's requirements in mind.

However, I realized that my new home came with additional responsibilities—cleaning, maintaining, and managing. *Well, I managed the whole nine yards back in America*, I thought. My two-bedroom Mumbai apartment seemed effortless compared to my four-bedroom Denver house spread over two stories and a walkout basement. Moreover, unlike America, where maids are very expensive, India has a sizable workforce available for these jobs, and at a considerably lower cost. This makes having daily household help economically feasible even for the middle class. I felt so relieved that I could find an affordable maid who would regularly come to clean my home; it was a relaxing feeling after doing everything on our own in America. Mumbai has perpetual construction projects, traffic, and pollution problems much more severe than what we experienced in Denver. So, the dust finds a way and accumulates daily inside the homes, and even though ours was a two-bedroom apartment, daily cleaning was too much hassle.

In my mind, I had already envisioned the maid's schedule: arriving at eight-thirty a.m. and staying until ten thirty, cleaning dishes, mopping, dusting furniture, and folding laundry. Then she would come again around four p.m. to wash the lunch dishes and clean the kitchen. It seemed like the perfect plan; well suited to my family's needs.

One of our building security guards supplied the maids' contact numbers, just like a diligent placement agent. He assured me he would send someone that afternoon. But evening arrived, and no one had shown up. Desperate for help, I thought I should have packed my vacuum cleaner with the other appliances I had shipped to India. Using the Indian broom was very difficult for my out-of-practice and tired back.

The following day, the guard called. "Madam, I'm sending up a maid. See if you want to hire her."

I thought reflexively, *There is no doubt in my mind; why shouldn't I?* And I happily answered the buzzing doorbell.

I opened the door to a woman with a ruffled look. She was in her late twenties and looked like a new arrival from a different state; I was guessing a Northern state but was unsure. She wore a cotton *saree* and had pulled her *pallu*—the loose end of the *saree*—over her head just enough to cover her hair bun, leaving all the windswept hair falling on her forehead. She said something in her limited Hindi. The only word I followed was "guards."

I quickly understood what the security guard had meant earlier. Still, I asked her name and what she knew about apartment housework.

She answered, "Salima," and said nothing else.

I was disappointed and couldn't hire her—Salima's lack of Hindi communication skills would make it difficult to describe the job to her.

Unlike America, there were no machines to help with sweeping and mopping. Some vacuum cleaners were available, but no iRobots for floors. Moreover, there was no time for research as soon as we moved in. In 2009, there were still no dishwashers available, and the apartments were not even wired for dishwashers, so in later years, when we finally did get a dishwasher, we had to install additional electrical wiring.

With so much daily housework to manage, I was overwhelmed and frustrated. The only solution was to hire help as soon as possible. I also believed in the fantasy that, with the right help, I would gain more free time so I could focus peacefully on my work while the help kept the apartment clean and functional.

The next day, the guards sent a new maid early in the morning. I happily answered the door to a thirty-year-old woman in a *saree*. A little quiet but with a firm look, she told me her name, Tulsi, and showed me an identity card issued by our building complex.

"How long have you been working here?"

"*Mai saat saal se kaam kar raahi hun,*" Tulsi answered instantly.

I was happy and relieved that she communicated well in Hindi and had seven years of work experience. We discussed her pay, and I asked that she start immediately. But while explaining the dos and don'ts in the house, I noticed she acted as if she was hearing them for the first time. I was certain she must have heard these instructions several times elsewhere. Still, when I left the housework to her the next day, I was delighted to return to my laptop. *Finally, I can get some of my own work done.*

A mere thirty minutes later, Tulsi returned and asked, "Where is the broom and the mop?"

"I showed you yesterday," I replied, but her face showed no recollection of our prior conversation. Leaving my laptop open, I got up and explained everything again. Fifteen minutes later, Tulsi came back—this time, asking for the washing machine instructions and wanting me to demonstrate how I wanted my laundry folded. *But she has seven years' experience,* I reminded myself.

Eventually, within the short span of two weeks, all the dos and don'ts were flexed. Tulsi started coming at ten instead of eight-thirty, worked only until eleven, and returned for the remaining work at twelve. Soon, the whole household functioned in a way that was convenient for Tulsi. I opted to just let it go since the mundane yet essential tasks in the house were carried out regularly. Also, I didn't want to lose her, as I was thinking about a long-term association.

It had been so different in my childhood where we treated the housemaids like family. Mom even helped with their kids' education or sometimes lent them money to buy a new hut for their family. Other times, she paid for their medicine and doctors' visits. So, I had always hoped to have the maid with us long term, almost like a family member. Ironically, Tulsi appeared to believe in the opposite, focusing only on the present and relying on that month's salary. I was bewildered by that thinking, and eventually, for my own understanding, I began to categorize the maids I had hired in the tower culture of the suburbs, based on their work ethics, so I would know how to function around them in the future.

One day, our second maid, Alima, agonized over her pain when she saw me sitting on the sofa and started chatting, assuming my downtime signaled I was available for chitchat.

"Didi ("older sister"—what the maids called the female members of the households where they worked), do you know the house where I work in C building," Alima continued, "she makes me work so much more. If her husband is in any of the rooms, I cannot enter that room to clean. I have to wait outside until her husband exits, and only then can I clean the room. This way, I unnecessarily spend so much additional time at her house and work till I almost drop. But that Madam never even offers me tea or coffee." Sitting in my kitchen, Alima recounted her story while munching on snacks and tea.

She regularly complained that in other houses, she had to work at so many different tasks, like wiping the doors, the kitchen windowsills, etc., even though the person explicitly hired for dusting was responsible for these duties. I suspected the point of her complaint was not to condemn the other employers but to plant the idea in my mind so that I would be aware, and therefore, refrain from making her regular workload any heavier. Nonetheless, she expected a hefty payment for the same amount of work.

The third maid I hired was Laatifah, who spent enough time on her work the first two weeks. But she quickly grew comfortable and began gradually cutting corners so that by her third week, the work that had previously taken her two hours to complete got done within an hour. And before I could question her, she bustled around and exited the apartment to move on to the next one. The washed dishes might have soap scum on them, the mopped floor might still have trash in the corners, and sometimes, the room not used regularly ended up neglected. Whenever I confronted her, she just went into the room again, feigned an effort to redo things, and rushed out the door saying, "Ho gaya," which means completed . . . but in this case, in name only.

So, after these three maids, I realized that, in Mumbai, the job of quality control rested on me, and there was no one to complain to. I ended up talking to Laatifah, who just shrugged and asked, "Why are you always questioning? Work in your house is too much."

Disheartened, I thought of the maid services I'd hired to clean my house in America every ten days. When I explained the requirements to their manager, they were trained accordingly and knew their job. If the work was unsatisfactory, I could call their company and they would address it by sending someone else the very next day.

"But you can't compare them with Mumbai maids," Neeraj countered. "The agencies in Denver used to charge eighty-five dollars for one visit."

"That's true, and they didn't do laundry or wash the dishes either," I acknowledged.

Fortunately, we later found two terrific maids for our house who would come on time, cook delicious food, and work diligently.

Still, whenever one of the maids was on-site, I had to be available to find the mop or a broom or search for the right kind of vegetable-cutting knife while she stood tapping her fingers on the kitchen counter. Sometimes, I had to lend her my cell phone so she could place a call. Every time I fielded one of these interruptions and returned to my laptop, the documents on the screen, particularly my job applications, were still there, waiting for me to complete them. I realized that having a maid was not as time-freeing as I had hoped;

it took much of my time just to manage the help. I grew frustrated and defeatedly tossed away my hope of resting and not lifting a finger while having a maid in the house.

However, I still wondered if I might not have communicated well with the maids and should perhaps learn those skills to avoid similar confusion in the future.

A few years later, in 2014, the opportunity presented itself, and I was able to test that idea. Ronak barely needed me to drive him around for school and other activities, as he was now older and gladly took an autorickshaw for his daily commute. So, I took this opportunity to concentrate on a business development plan for our company and began investing time and money in programs on personal growth and business enhancement. As part of our learning exercises, motivational and self-help books and business management guides topped my reading list in those days. Being a psychology student and a business owner, I was naturally inclined to learn more about interpersonal aspects and clear guidance for managers. I was painstakingly focused on learning effective communication with my staff. Those principles had benefited me with my coworkers and subordinates at work, so I hoped they'd work in other scenarios as well.

Of course, during those days, working from home barely had any boundaries for me. I felt caught in the middle, squeezed between the overlapping responsibilities of home and work. Consequently, I was tempted every day to try out the managerial principles I was learning—not in my work environment but with my home help.

One day, I was able to practice my patience and managerial skills with my maid. Rashida had been absent for four consecutive days without informing me. On the morning of the fifth day, she rang the bell, and as I partially opened the door, Rashida, a little heavy-set, in her mid-thirties, wearing a neatly draped and pinned-up *saree*, hair tied over her nape, stood there awkwardly.

"Where were you for the last four days, Rashida?" I darted the question through my half-open door.

Avoiding eye contact and not replying, she squeezed through the door, entered the kitchen, and immediately began scrubbing the dishes.

Ronak and Neeraj were in the living room, so I refrained from making a scene. Quietly rolling my eyes, I cautiously followed her into the kitchen. "Where were you, Rashida?" Carefully exerting my patience, I asked again.

Rashida kept the tap water running and slowly turned the utensils upside down in the sink without lifting her eyes. I frowned but told myself to handle the situation like a professional.

Management principles suggest that mostly all problems are preventable if you communicate well, and early, so I decided to communicate. These management books also recommended admonishing insubordination as part of effective communication and further suggested looking at your subordinate while issuing a warning. "Rashida, please pay attention when I am talking to you," I said in a softer tone.

This time, she complied and stopped scrubbing the dishes. However, still looking down, she avoided eye contact while fidgeting with her *saree*.

"Where were you for the last four days? Tell me, Rashida." Annoyed, I asked again.

Finally, she answered briefly, "Didi, I had a fever, and my child was ill too."

"Oh, I'm sorry to hear that. How are you now? And what kind of fever was it?"

"I'm okay now, but my child is still sick," she answered.

"I hope your child gets well soon. But why didn't you call me? That's all I ask. If you have to miss work one day, phone me and hang up before I answer, and I will call you back; you don't have to spend money on the call. But I must know if you are not coming to work so that I can make alternate arrangements."

Rashida lifted her eyes momentarily with what seemed like repentance until she looked away.

Making my voice stern, I confronted her for insubordination. "You chose not to call me and didn't even pick up my calls. Why?"

"No, Didi. We did not receive any calls since my husband kept the phone with him at work, and I was sleeping at home with a fever." She briefly looked up sheepishly.

I was running out of patience, so before I dived in, I recalled the steps and decided to experiment with those principles. I had learned that you must explain what the subordinate did wrong. Also, tell them how you feel about this experience and let the message register properly. Then, convey to the subordinate that you value them. So, first, I looked her straight in the eyes. "Rashida, you made a mistake by not informing me about your four days off. No one expects you to work if you are ill. But I needed to know, at least." I went on to present my case rationally. "While you were out, the first day and the second day, I waited till three p.m. for you, and then along with my work, I had to pick up all the housework myself. It was very tiring, as I was doing my job and your work too. I could have made alternate arrangements if I had known you were going to miss work."

Rashida seemed unaffected by this.

Then, still following the management principles, I looked at her in silence to let my message sink in. I thought I would hear an apology, as I probably would have heard in any professional environment. Rashida, however, was quiet. Finally, I exhaled, lightly patted her shoulder, and said, "I am disappointed, but I like your work, and I hope you won't repeat the same mistake next time. Just one missed call would suffice."

She pressed her lips together, flashed a tight-lipped smile, and resumed scrubbing the dishes hastily. Taking my cue, I made myself scarce.

I felt a little confused, as the response I would have received from a professional subordinate would have involved communication, but Rashida had offered only a subdued smile. Yet I felt lighter after conveying my feelings effectively without losing my patience.

As our software consultants were hired to work with us from remote locations, I communicated with them remotely. I did not see any issues in their communication, even though it was not face-to-face. But Rashida was a woman who lacked education and likely lived a hand-to-mouth existence. So, I never expected any out-of-the-ordinary response from her. However, I at least expected an apology. Instead, after mopping my apartment that day, Rashida said, "I am running late, Didi, and you wanted to talk, so I wasted more time there. I am getting late for my next job, so I will do your remaining work in the evening, once I finish all my work today."

Baffled, I could only say, "Okay."

When she showed up in the evening, she asked for the money to pay the doctor's bill for her little one. So, sympathetically, I paid her entire month's salary in advance and told her not to worry.

Nevertheless, Rashida did not come the following day or the days after either; she never even picked up my phone calls after that. And then I realized that although I had thought I was very effective in communicating and even applied management principles while doing so, our conversation hadn't had the desired effect.

Later, I learned that she had wanted to test the waters as a full-time maid at another employer's house and had worked there for those four days while remaining absent from my home. Also, she had faked her illness to get that advance payment from me. I was shocked by this manipulation and bewildered by her lies.

Distressed and disheartened, I discussed this experience with my lecturer; he laughed and joked, "You can't test management principles on your maid." He added, "Because of their situation, people who do those jobs don't think twice if they are offered something slightly better."

I was speechless.

He went on to advise that he never used his expertise in such matters and tried to keep the help in his house very happy by paying them incentives or bonuses. He claimed that if he didn't, they'd leave sooner rather than later, for sure.

"So much for effective communication!" I said ruefully.

After this debacle, I concluded that, although these management principles helped me professionally, and my communication was impeccable, they offered zero assistance in managing my household help. Lesson learned: As my lecturer advised, *Don't ever test management principles on your maid!*

Despite the issues with some of our household help, over a period of time, we also had some maids who were very kind and great human beings. There was Rakilla, who came every afternoon to wash the cookware and clean the kitchen. If I was down with back pain, she would sympathetically massage my back and feet with oil without regard for her own time and never expected any money in exchange. Then there was Noorie, who never worked as a cook in my house but cleaned the office apartment we rented for a while, yet she brought me mutton *biryani* and *kheer* that she'd cooked for her Eid Festival celebration. Additionally, there was Alima, who, despite her other work, never moved our time and kept coming punctually because she knew that I would start my office work after eleven a.m. And I recall Noorjahan, who never complained, in spite of the heavy load of cookware and dishes she had to wash on the days our friends or family visited us for lunch.

After hiring many maids and cooks, I concluded that my family was a different type entirely. Most importantly, Neeraj worked from home at night while in India. So, he needed space and quiet hours during the day to catch up on sleep. Therefore, we needed the maids to complete their work during their allotted two-to-three-hour shifts and then leave for the day. Besides, Neeraj grew up in a household with no maids. So, having full-time maids working twenty-four hours a day, seven days a week, in our house would have been very cumbersome for him.

I realized that in my parents' home, I had been responsible for only my job and a few chores, as we had maids. So, the first time I came to the U.S., I had to take care of my work, get used to cooking most of our meals in an American kitchen, and split the housework duties with my spouse because that was the American custom. So, after taking care of the household chores yourself, you get used to doing the tasks a certain way. And even though I wished for additional help with cooking and housework, once I was back in Mumbai, I was not ready to give the reins entirely to someone else. I stayed invested in the cooking and nutrition and delegated the baseline work to the maids. I was disappointed when I didn't see cleanliness and a reasonable level of diligence, but I also realized that perhaps their grueling work schedules, which involved working at several houses each day, had an impact on the overall quality of their work.

16

The Price for Being American

"We are from Bengaluru," I told the new maid one day. I had good reason for fudging the truth. Within the first six months of settling into our apartment, we realized some people and businesses—may they be carpenters, maids, vegetable vendors, or even a goldsmith—demanded more money from us once they knew we had come from outside India.

They always assumed that we could afford more since we were from overseas. They demanded premium payment while delivering the same goods or services for which they charged less to others. In response, we chose to downplay our recent arrival in India and presented ourselves as being from the city of Bengaluru. This Southern city helped us justify the status of new-to-Mumbai written all over our faces and keep costs more reasonable.

Examples of this dynamic were many. I distinctly remember we received the keys to our new apartment in 2008 but couldn't move in for a year. When I visited in 2009, I noticed cobwebs on the ceiling. So, I called housekeeping and asked how much it would cost to have someone mop the floor with soap and water and clear the cobwebs.

"Five hundred rupees," the man replied.

That sounded expensive, but I assumed it was their regular rate. The man I spoke with arrived with two uniformed staff during their lunch hour and, within fifteen minutes, washed the entire floor with nothing but water, hastily swishing the straw broom over the wet surface. By the time I looked over the entire apartment, they had finished and were waiting in the doorway for payment. I gave them five Rs 100 notes, and they happily departed. When I returned to Mom's place, she told me, "They must have said five hundred rupees for the month."

"No," I argued. "I clearly said I needed cleaning today."

"But for a house with no furniture and bare walls, five hundred rupees for an entire month's cleaning is still too much," Mom insisted.

I was dumbfounded, realizing I hadn't comprehended the value of Rs 500. "Mom, back in the States, my maids came every ten days, charging eighty-five dollars a visit. I said yes to his offer based on that. Besides, he was available immediately; otherwise, where would I find help for my locked apartment?"

After talking with Mom, I suspected the housekeeping man had pictured a not-used-to-Mumbai sign on my face. Or maybe I was unfamiliar with the new Mumbai, and my negotiating skills had gotten rusty. Either way, there was no point beating myself up over it. But for future reference, I made a mental note to "always negotiate" or ask around about the prevailing rates for goods and services.

CR

17

Sampling the Food Culture of Mumbai

"When in Rome, do as the Romans do," my dad always said on family vacations, especially when encouraging us kids to be adventurous in sampling the specialty cuisine of that location. One of my motivations for returning to India was being able to sample excellent and authentic Indian food at our convenience, and so I figured, what better way to experience Mumbai life than satisfying our taste buds with tempting, sizzling, spicy, and delicious treats?

Indian restaurants back in the Mile High City closed by nine p.m. Being on a laid-back schedule after a long workday, we usually began our evening chai time at seven, so bringing the family to an Indian restaurant before nine was a challenge. After the move, I was pleased to learn that Mumbai restaurants stayed open until midnight, and many people arrived for dinner after ten p.m.

The city's food culture is quite dynamic and inclusive, allowing us to sample foods from different eras and parts of India. It's a culinary heaven of authentic platters of Malwani, Marathi, Goan, and Southern food, among others. Mughlai, Punjabi, and Portuguese dishes are equally revered. Also, the competition between regional fusion dishes and international fast foods is always vying for the attention of food connoisseurs all over the city.

Surrounded by the Arabian Sea, Mumbai is also a seafood hub known for fresh and a wide variety of exotic fish like Bombay duck, mackerel, and crabs, among others. Neeraj had become vegetarian before we married, but postmove, that never stopped him from going to the local fish market in the mornings and buying pomfret and prawns, Ronak's favorite seafood. Neeraj was a popular customer in the Malad Fish Market because he never bargained and would buy the fish at any price they quoted. Once home, like a professional chef, he would salt, wash, and marinate the fish and then shallow fry it, just the way Ronak liked it.

Even though we cooked fish at home, we never stopped seeking out specialty seafood restaurants in Mumbai. In fact, we searched for opportunities to savor the local seafood. One day, I took my harmonium for servicing, bringing Ronak with me to the center of Mumbai. It was almost noon when we dropped off the instrument and were immediately caught in a monsoon rain. We looked around the busy street: The rain slowed the traffic, the wandering wind scattered the rainfall, and the cool breeze wafted across my face. Of course, we had to forgive potholes on the roads, full of murky water.

We decided to take refuge at a famous nearby restaurant until the storm subsided. This midsize restaurant was in Dadar West and was named after a district in the Konkan Region, my parents' ancestral homeland in coastal Maharashtra. Just the thought of the food of this region made my mouth water. We glanced over the menu and felt obligated to order almost everything.

Eventually, a plate of three sizzling *bombil fry* with hot, steaming *fulkas* was placed in front of us. The aroma of spicy fried Bombay duck fish and ghee-covered Indian flatbread entirely consumed us on that cold rainy afternoon. But, to our astonishment, the food remained in the dish for only a few minutes before it melted on our tongues and disappeared into our mouths. The icing on the cake was the relatively quick service when we ordered four more plates of *bombil fry* with clam *masala* curry to dip the *rotis* in the delicious bowl of clams in coconut gravy. At the end of the meal, we ordered *sol-kadhi*, traditionally consumed in Konkan to boost digestion after a heavy meal of fried spiced seafood. It's a perfect blend of *kokum*—a sour fruit extract—with coconut milk, complemented with just the right number of green chilies and cilantro. Satisfied and overstuffed, when we received our bill, we were baffled to find we didn't need deep pockets to enjoy tasty food in India.

On another occasion, we joined my cousin and his family for good tandoor seafood delicacies at a restaurant in Parle. After an hour-long wait outside the restaurant, we finally went in. The place was a little stuffy, but the tempting aroma teased our taste buds and challenged our hunger pangs, so we were just glad to get a table. We unanimously decided on crab tandoori and several of their other seafood specialties. Soon, we got busy munching on the delicious fish-fry appetizers. A waiter appeared with three giant live crabs on a large tray. Not knowing why he was bringing live crabs to our table, we furrowed our brows at my cousin, who pointed at the biggest one on the tray and selected it as our crab tandoori dish. It made us feel special to choose the actual seafood before they cooked our meal.

Although Neeraj loathed going out in traffic, especially after work-from-home assignments, we explored all the nearby restaurants. We tried the Marriott and Westin, as they had valet parking, and their buffet restaurants were our favorite destinations for

Sunday brunches. Although these were a little pricey, one could find continental, Indian, Mughlai, and American grills at the same buffet. It was a blessing to us, as Ronak missed American grill options, mainly salmon entrées, far away from America. We were glad to see those options readily available. The buffets' elaborate dessert spreads were perfect blends of East meets West, where *kheer, gulab jamun,* and *jalebi,* prepared in pure clarified butter, were perched royally alongside bite-size cakes, pastries, and ice creams.

"This is my kind of restaurant," Ronak declared on reaching the buffet at the Marriott Hotel for the first time. The chefs were more than happy to prepare something that wasn't offered at the buffet and readily whipped up smoked salmon for Ronak.

Ronak filled up on salmon, chicken *tikka,* chicken tandoori, and assorted *naan* and then cornered the dessert section. Neeraj and I were delighted with their *chatpata* (spicy and tangy) appetizers, which included *sev puri, batata vada,* and *papadi chaat.* I would insatiably fill my plate with these appetizers, then make a trip to the salad bar to devour all their fresh salads and soups.

Fast Food

Back in the mid-80s, when my mom's telephone exchange office was at Andheri West, occasionally, she would take us to the famous bakery near that place. It was owned by a Parsi family and was well known for its cakes, pastries, and pizzas. They served pizza in only one size, comparable to today's personal-size pizzas in America, with tomato-chili sauce topped with tomatoes, onions, green peppers, and Amul cheese. But the feeling that we could taste something contemporary, riding the fast-food fad in those days, was a pleasant experience for us, kids.

We learned about burgers around the early 90s, when Rupert

Murdoch's media network descended upon Mumbai. We could see American culture and food through Hollywood movies and soap operas and could find fast-food joints like McDonald's only in those films.

In contrast, today's Mumbai is filled with international fast-food chains. The Mumbai residents have developed a great appetite for both the Indian version of fast food as well as American fast food, and they happily relish Bombay sandwiches and *vada pav* along with pizzas and burgers.

Are You from Mars?

Over time, we started observing a kind of negligence in some restaurants, and instead of arguing with restaurant employees, we made a list of sites to avoid. But surprisingly, some people dining with us would judge us for our health and safety concerns.

"Are you from Mars?" a very snobbish relative of mine asked me at a restaurant's inauguration ceremony.

For a minute, I was dumbfounded. Then I started processing the accusation in her tone and wondered if I was doing something wrong. All this pushback just for asking about the safety protocols and hygiene regimen being followed in the restaurant? I had no intention of criticizing their business practices; I only wanted to determine whether the site and its food were suitable for me and my child to consume.

This person's voice kept ringing in my ears. There is nothing wrong with being conscious about health and the food we eat. Especially when you are a mom; that's the first criterion you consider whenever your child is around food: "Is it safe to consume?"

"I can't forgo the knowledge I have acquired over a long period concerning the care and safety measures in the food industry," I argued. "I cannot unlearn what I know works for my family."

I also noticed that people tried to guilt-trip me for being insensitive if I asked about safety measures. After our move to India, I managed to find and connect with my college friends through the blessing of social media. We would all meet up for birthday celebrations and reminisce over college memories. One of those friends invited us to a restaurant at a mall for one such birthday celebration. The friend intended to order a few dishes to share, and we all decided to go with the flow. When I ordered bottled water, a few raised their eyebrows. But one adamant soul was hell-bent on judging me. "I don't understand you foreigners. Why do you unnecessarily order bottled water?" Her tone was accusatory.

"Look at the water jugs they have placed openly," I offered. "No one handling them seems to be doing it carefully, and we are already in monsoon season."

"If you are so picky, why did you come to India?" she lashed out. "Go back to America."

Incredulous, I thought she was arguing as if she were feeding me my daily bread and butter. "In the first place, I never told you my reservations about the water. You raised that issue, and now, you're judging me, and you're not even paying for the water," I answered, keeping my cool. Water is vital, and during monsoons, there is a higher risk of contamination; I remember in my childhood, Mom always boiled the drinking water during monsoons.

Neeraj and I faced multiple such situations and careless restaurants, so we preferred five-star restaurant buffets for our family. The buffet spreads were lavish and elaborate with the perfect mix of Indian and continental dishes. Most importantly, quality control checks were always in place so that one could expect clean and delicious food without a need to apologize to judgmental, so-called friends.

ॐ

18

Caught between Denim and *Salwar Kurta*

I had promised myself that once we were settled in Mumbai, I would purchase more Indian clothing. Indian attire has always fascinated me with its vibrant colors and detailed weaves, designs, and fabric textures. So, I was quite surprised to find, after our arrival, that Punjabi dresses or *sarees* were no longer common choices, as a majority of women in the city now seemed to prefer typical Western clothing.

I favored clothes that were trendy yet comfortable, given Mumbai's hot, humid climate, but the availability of malls around that area also influenced my choices. Now that I was free of Colorado's freezing temperatures, colorful cotton casuals seemed like fresh air. In Mumbai, my printed indigo cotton dress was enough without the additional layer of a jacket.

When Neeraj and I worked as IT professionals in Colorado, we mostly dressed in business casual on weekdays and wore jeans with a casual top on weekends. The exceptions were weekends when we had a Desi event to attend—a birthday party, a festival celebration at the temple, or a potluck get-together at some Desi house. Since

I regretted not being able to wear Indian outfits to work, I enjoyed wearing Indian dresses or *sarees* for such weekend invites. As our family was invited to Indian events almost every weekend, I wore my Indian outfits at least fifty times a year back in Colorado.

After returning to Mumbai, we received invitations mainly from family and extended family. I loved pairing a raw silk *salwar kurta* (pants and long tunic) in a contrasting color with an ikat *dupatta* (scarf). But I soon found myself sweating profusely in that silk combination due to the heat. Eventually, for relief, I would change into comfortable denim capris with thin, ethnic-printed tunics. So, I rarely wore traditional Indian outfits in Mumbai, which made me feel a bit guilty until I realized the Western part of the city boasted mostly contemporary clothing.

In our first year, for the Dussehra Festival celebrations, I wanted to buy customary marigold garlands for the door decoration and *puja* (worship ritual). I remembered, as a child, visiting the central market at Goregaon Station with Dad to buy *puja* materials like incense candles, camphor, sweets, and fruits. We always returned home on the bus with many shopping bags. Of course, in our first year after the move, Neeraj and I did not own a car, so, with great difficulty, I found an autorickshaw to drive me to the same market near Goregaon Station. I knew that one should wear mainly full-body-covering clothes to avoid funny stares from some people in the marketplace. So I wore jeans and a cotton top with mega-sleeves and a Chinese collar; but at the market, I realized that the shopkeepers were looking at me quizzically. What was it?

That look in their eyes—was it curiosity? But why would it be? I assumed they regularly saw some girls working in the offices wearing trousers to their workplaces or female students dressed in jeans. It seemed they were looking at me as an outsider, not part of this market. Then again, maybe I was just imagining it. And then it hit me—none of the women my age were wearing Western clothes. Apparently, I did not conform to the stereotypes. All the thirty-something women who were returning from work and exiting the train station wore *sarees*; a few wore Punjabi dresses. I also noticed that many ladies from a lower class, who wore crumpled cotton *sarees*, were buying from these hawkers. Plus, with my outfit so different, vendors didn't see me as a buying customer; perhaps they thought I was just there to inquire and compare prices and not buy from them, as I did not look like their idea of a customer. Suddenly, I also felt like I was in the wrong market.

I realized that the bazaar I used to visit with Dad in the past did not belong to people like us anymore. If Dad were alive, he also would have refrained from visiting. With the advent of big airconditioned grocery stores and small local vegetable markets, not many from my area traveled to Goregaon Station Market anymore. I noticed that other customers asked about the prices and quickly started to haggle with the vegetable vendors. But when I asked for a price, the vendors would skeptically quote me a number. And since the vegetables were locally grown, and I found them relatively cheaper in rupees, I rarely haggled with the vendors; plus, I was out of practice in my bargaining skills, so I just paid the prices they quoted. I think that gave away my ignorance, and I thought, with my lack of bargaining, the vendors had less respect for me, despite taking more money from me.

But even though I preferred buying at big grocery stores for convenience, some typical local green vegetables like *alu* and *mayalu*, and fruits like *jambhul*, black currants, and ice apple were available only in the markets near the station road.

Later, my modest, printed cotton *kurtas* and plain *salwar* with my ponytail hairstyle came to my rescue whenever I wandered off to the local markets for fresh green vegetables. I feel that the casual Indian outfit helped me blend in perfectly.

CR

19

Festivals Add Colors to Life

My colorful rangoli.

I woke up around four thirty a.m. to Neeraj's tap on my shoulder; he flashed a smile and wished, "Happy Diwali!"

"I wish you the same. I am so happy it's Diwali."

Diwali had always brought me joy, whether I celebrated it in my parents' house or with Neeraj and Ronak in Denver, however this was the first Diwali in our new Mumbai apartment, and we were all ecstatic.

Enthusiastically, to help us get into the festive mood, I had already bought many terra-cotta lamps to color with intricate designs in vibrant hues. We would light them in our home during this festival, and the remaining *diyas* would accompany the boxes of sweets we gifted to friends and family during the holidays. For the past fifteen days, I had shopped for new clothes, unique gifts for everyone, decorations, and a wide variety of sweets for ourselves. Simultaneously, I was occupied in the kitchen making traditional Diwali sweets, the sweet and savory types of snacks my mom prepared in my childhood. After all, they say this celebration cannot be complete without traditional homemade sweets. So, I was glad that I learned about a place in Goregaon where women small-business owners prepared and sold homemade Marathi sweets and snacks year-round. That made it easier for me to prepare a few for *shakun* (good luck) at home and order the rest.

"I finished coloring all the remaining *diyas* last night," I said proudly, pointing at the tray decorated with marigold flowers and *diyas* on the coffee table. *So much for the joy of giving*, Neeraj must have thought. Excited, I had made many trips to the potters for the small terra-cotta lamps. Considering the cost of petrol consumed each time, those Rs 10 terra-cotta lamps probably amounted to about Rs 100 each. "It looks great!" he answered instead.

Neeraj had bought four giant lanterns so we could hang one on each room's balcony, and we made one more trip to the market for colorful electric string lights to hang as well.

Enthusiastic about our first Diwali celebration in Mumbai, Ronak demanded string lights to match the blue-and-white lantern he had picked for his balcony. "I am so glad I can finally put lights in my room and on my balcony this year." He reminded us of his multiple requests in the past to decorate his room with lights on the second floor of our Colorado house. Although the lights were placed mainly over the house roofline and porch railing, we kept the individual rooms clear due to potential fire hazards. But our Mumbai apartment, having an independent balcony for his room, posed no obstacle in that concrete building; he could have the lights and a lantern for his balcony.

When our family visited the market a week before Diwali, it was a customary Diwali bazaar. Overflowing with people, products, shops, and hawkers everywhere on the roads, the bazaar was bursting with festive colors, colorful clothes, drapes, and bright new appliances, among other wares. Several street vendors sat selling *rangoli* (colors, stencils, and pattern books), *diyas*, lanterns, heaps of marigold flowers and garlands, fruits, and vegetables right outside the permanent shops, making the roads look vibrantly colorful. Pop-up shops carrying Diwali crackers sprouted everywhere. The streets were so crowded that instead of making their way to the shops, people preferred buying products from the hawkers, both to save time and to hone their bargaining skills. The sweetshops featured specialty dried-fruit sweets—candies shaped like miniature watermelons, apples, and strawberries, made of cashews, almonds, and pistachios. There were *paan* candies and *paneer* sweets made only for Diwali, in addition to the usual line of *motichur laddu* and *mawa mithai*.

This festival indeed demanded a parade of seasonal jobs in Mumbai! Diwali also helped small-business owners prosper. Looking at the colorful strategic displays of string lights at the shops, Ronak picked out his favorite. I chose identical vibrant yellow lights for our home. Quickly realizing my color theme, Neeraj reminded me, "We live in a twenty-story apartment building, and most apartments will have string lights on their balconies. So, our single-tone lights will appear dull when compared with others."

"Yes, good point," I mused. "Let's go with bright red and yellow." Finally, I realized Diwali is a festival of lights and colors, celebrated across India. So, we had to mix and match colors to stand out.

Like a kid in a toy shop, Ronak curiously observed as the shop-keeper packed our lights. "Made in China?" Ronak almost screamed as he read the information on the light boxes.

Wide-eyed, not knowing how to react, I gazed at Neeraj for help. "Use your indoor voice, Ronak," I suggested, frowning.

Seated on the barstool the shopkeeper had kindly brought out to make his young customer comfortable, Ronak couldn't contain his bewilderment. "Even in India, we are buying made-in-China products?"

"If the product is good, why not?" Neeraj finally came to my rescue.

"No, Dad! Our history teacher suggested that we should buy products made in India during festivals to help our country." Now, Ronak's outburst made sense.

"Excellent point, Ronak! Let's buy Indian-made lights," I agreed, asking the shopkeeper to show us the Indian-made ones instead.

A little hesitant, the shopkeeper exchanged a look with his sales-man, who explained that, while they had red, blue, and green, my choice of bright yellow was not available in Indian-made.

Well then, I thought, *I am focused only on the colors' brightness and the decoration that will bring happiness to my family during Diwali, not on the product's brand or national origin.* I quietly processed this, as I was not ready to own up to my hypocrisy in front of my child, especially in his formative years. So, we compromised by purchasing a combination of blue, green, yellow, and red string lights, both Indian and Chinese-made.

Over the next three days, Neeraj and Ronak decorated each bedroom balcony with different colorful string lights, complemented by a giant lantern on each balcony. "Each gallery looks like a separate room now." Ronak admired the lantern hung over his bedroom balcony.

Finally, after a week's worth of preparations, I couldn't help but smile on that Diwali morning. After all, I would be celebrating this festival of lights in my motherland after twelve years; I had once traveled to India during Diwali when Ronak was just a year old.

"Indeed, a very happy Diwali and our first one together in India," Neeraj said, exiting the bedroom to make morning chai.

It was still dark outside at five a.m., so he immediately switched on the lantern and string of lights on the living room balcony.

"Neeraj, before chai, we must prepare for the Diwali *puja* celebration," I reminded him as I entered the kitchen. The first task was always sweeping the apartment. Then, I quickly added cotton wicks and oil to the terra-cotta *diyas* and woke up Ronak once all the prep work was finished.

"Happy Diwali, Ronak," I whispered in his ear. That mere whisper woke him, unlike every other day when I had to put in triple the effort to wake him for school. "May this Diwali bring you happiness, health, and prosperity!"

Wishing me a happy Diwali, he hugged me. "I want to light all the oil *diyas* today."

"Sure, after you help me with *rangoli* in front of our main door."

Neeraj wished Ronak a happy Diwali as he switched on the lantern and string lights on Ronak's balcony. As Ronak and I joined him on the balcony, the sky was still dark, and the balcony looked starlit.

"It's five a.m. on Diwali morning, and I still haven't heard any firecrackers bursting in our complex," Neeraj said, sounding somewhat concerned.

"You're right," I acknowledged, "but I can hear firecrackers in the distance."

"So what, Dad? We can be the first to light the fireworks in our complex," Ronak suggested eagerly.

"Ronak, on this auspicious day, you can set off firecrackers only if you shower, followed by morning prayers, and then eat our customary breakfast," I said, carefully listing the rituals of Diwali morning.

"Mom, you forgot *rangoli* outside the door, flower garlands to decorate the front door, and God's *mandir*." Ronak sounded like an expert after those years of Diwali celebrations he'd experienced during his early childhood. Neeraj and I had big smiles on our faces to hear our offspring, who, by now, knew our customs well, being so attentive to the family traditions.

It took an hour and a half for the three of us to get ready in our brand-new festive clothes, complete the *puja*, and take our places at the table for breakfast. We sampled homemade, nutritious Diwali sweets and savory snacks with our morning tea.

"Mom, it's six thirty a.m., and I still can't hear firecrackers. Maybe they aren't allowed here," Ronak speculated.

I wondered too. "Growing up in Mumbai, we always heard the deafening firecracker noises beginning at four a.m. on Diwali mornings. By six-thirty, the roads were filled with leftover papers, half-burnt crackers, and firework ash."

"Ronak, it's Diwali, and in India, no one will object to fireworks," Neeraj assured him. "Let's go down in the open area to light the firecrackers."

I agreed as it was Ronak's first-ever experience with so many different firecrackers. Like any parents, we wanted to enjoy Diwali through his eyes. But I glanced sideways at Neeraj, and he expressed his own puzzlement by frowning at me.

"It's a real surprise about the firecrackers, though," I whispered to him.

"Let's be the first to light them," Neeraj said as he gently picked up a few firecracker boxes and a matchbox to light the sparklers.

Surprisingly, when we reached the building's lobby, it was quiet too. We couldn't miss the perplexed look on the security guards' faces, seeing the whole family dressed in festive clothes early in the morning. Baffled, they kept looking at the firecrackers and the boxes of sweets in our hands. I presented both guards with *mithai* boxes and wished them happy Diwali.

"Thank you, Madam, for your pre-Diwali gift. Are you going out tomorrow on Diwali day?" he quipped.

"Who told you Diwali is tomorrow?" I frowned.

"In our villages, Laxmi *puja* will be celebrated tomorrow, per the calendar," he answered with a smirk. His eyes questioned how someone could celebrate Diwali early.

"Where is your village, Chandan?"

"I am from a small village near Moradabad in North India."

"Even my village is near Agra, but Diwali is tomorrow," Raamlal added for emphasis.

This instantly explained why we hadn't heard any fireworks nearby. Mostly, I recalled, the residents in our complex were from North India; I had barely seen any Marathi-speaking person in the complex. The states of Maharashtra, where Mumbai is located, Goa, and a few Southern parts of the country start the Diwali celebration on Narak Chaturdashi day.

"Mumbai always celebrates from the first day of Diwali, one day before Laxmi *puja*. Remember to give us your Diwali wishes today, or else you will not get any sweets from us," I jested as I walked out to join my family, hearing the guards' laughter in the background.

Exiting the building, I could feel the mild November chill and noticed Ronak preparing to light the *anaar* firework a few meters away. I had always loved lighting this type of firecracker, as it was less intense. I loved seeing its fascinating sparkles falling around like a miniature rain shower and it brought instant joy to my face every time. Yet the mother in me just couldn't refrain from issuing safety instructions. "Light it quickly and move right away," I warned.

Ronak carefully looked around before placing the *anaar* on the ground and lit it cautiously by placing a sparkler over the *anaar's* pointy string, then swiftly moved for cover. From where I stood, as the firework slowly showered sparkles, taking its fountain as high as ten feet, I could see Ronak's whole face brighten with a smile, shining many times brighter than the firecracker's glare.

Due to safety restrictions, we couldn't light any fireworks back in Colorado except on the Fourth of July. Nonetheless, I always felt guilt-ridden that our biggest festival, Diwali, was incomplete in the U.S. without fireworks. After all those years of guilt, to witness Ronak being able to set off the firecrackers independently with his own hands and enjoy it entirely was an exhilarating experience for us.

The rest of the day went by quickly in happy phone conversations, visiting Grandma, exchanging gifts, and loading sweets into our over-stuffed bellies. On our way back from Grandma's, we made sure to stop by the podium park to view our apartment, dazzling in the bright gleam. Each of our balconies flaunted lanterns and colorful string lights in a theme of its own on that first night of Diwali.

The following day, our family was woken up early by the loud, obnoxious firecracker noise beginning at five-thirty a.m.

"Well, finally, here is Orion Elevations welcoming Diwali,"

Neeraj whispered while turning over and going back to sleep.

"Better late than never." I smiled while browsing the Diwali messages on my cell phone. I relaxed since this day did not require the five-a.m. bath and *puja* as on the first day; on subsequent days, we celebrated on our usual schedule.

Eventually, Neeraj and I got up around eight a.m.; Ronak was still asleep. So, after breakfast, I sneaked out the main door and used my quiet time to make *rangoli*. As the maid arrived, I gave her a Diwali bonus—a month's pay and a box of sweets.

"Diwali mubarak ho, Didi!" my maid wished me in Hindi, smiling.

I was halfway through adding the colors to my *rangoli* design when Ronak joined me, insisting that he complete the rest. I happily agreed.

In the meantime, our neighbors stepped out in casual clothes, heading to the elevator in the corridor. The wife asked, "What are you drawing? Oh! It's Diwali?" and shrugged.

They were young newlyweds, a working couple. Even though it was their day off, I was still surprised by their casual reaction to Diwali.

I remember, back in America, I always insisted on going the whole nine yards during festivals, as we wanted Ronak to learn about our culture and the importance of festivals in our lives. When Ronak was about six years old, I distinctly remember the second day of Diwali Laxmi *puja*. Of course, for the Indian festivals, there was no day off from work and school in America. I had had a very challenging day at work, full of meetings. When Neeraj and I picked up Ronak from daycare in the evening, we both were tired. But as soon as we reached home, I rolled up my sleeves and started prepping the *puja* room. Although it was a cold fall night in Colorado, I quickly completed a small design of colorful *rangoli* before lighting up *diyas* outside the main door; as my mother always taught me, *rangoli* was imperative to welcome Goddess Laxmi on that auspicious day.

"We don't have to do the *rangoli*," Neeraj had said at the time, feeling the piercing cold wind as he opened the door.

"It's a custom, so it's necessary," I had replied, emphasizing how important it was to me. "This is the only way our son will learn our traditions!"

Neeraj knew he would have to let me win that argument as a mother. So, he decided to participate in the festivities. Eventually, we dressed Ronak in his winter jacket, warm sweatpants, and shoes to join me outside our main door on that freezing October evening. Ronak helped me place the lighted *diyas* on our cold concrete porch and also made a small *rangoli* of his own, next to mine; being an artist, he has always been a quick learner. For the Laxmi *puja* ceremony, when I took the gold ornaments and currency out of the safe, Ronak wondered why we placed the jewelry on the *puja* table.

Neeraj explained in his witty style, "Although the money does not represent actual Laxmi, it's the symbolism that counts for Hindus."

"We offer our prayers to Goddess Laxmi by offering flowers and gratitude for our wealth on this auspicious day," I added.

I had a massive grin on my face and a grand realization that all those stories and customs had been acutely inculcated in me at my father's insistence and both my parents' initiative. And there we were on that Diwali evening, passing on this cultural tradition to the next generation.

But now, returning to our second morning of that first Diwali in Mumbai, having emphasized so much and been so particular about the customs during his upbringing, Ronak was being asked an "ignorant question" by the neighbor, a young woman who was much older than he was. Ronak looked at me with wide eyes, a little contemptuous, but didn't say anything yet. After they caught the elevator and disappeared from our floor, Ronak remarked, "People don't care about Diwali as much here as we did even in America. You always told me people make a big deal about Diwali in India, and that lady didn't even know today is Diwali!"

I had not failed to notice her Western clothes and the casual tone in her voice as she shrugged and left. I felt odd; I thought maybe I was old and was confronting a new India that I did not recognize anymore. I couldn't fathom how a person did not wear Indian attire on Diwali. Growing up, wearing colorful and shiny festive outfits was a highlight of Diwali days for us, kids.

I didn't mind her cluelessness, but I certainly didn't appreciate her expression of ignorance around my child in his formative years. I felt the new India was changing fast, especially in metropolitan cities like Mumbai. What we deemed mandatory during festivals when I was growing up was no longer observed by many members of the younger generation.

Colorful lantern on our balcony.

ॐ

20

A Mirage of Work Opportunities

I t had been six months since Neeraj had joined us in Mumbai. After he arrived around the end of August 2009, he continued working online during the night hours to fulfill his current project assignment while he recovered from jet lag. He familiarized himself with our new apartment, which had been turned into his office for remote log-in even before we'd moved in. We were super impressed with the high-speed internet the service companies now offered in Mumbai, which would have been unthinkable just a few years earlier.

By December, once his existing project had concluded, Neeraj started networking with his ex-engineering friends; after all, he had graduated from VJTI's renowned Computer Engineering branch, and he had many friends in India's technology sector. He found a few leads through his friends' network and went through various job interviews with different job profiles in the software industry. After a few senior software position interviews, we realized that, unlike several American companies, these jobs required most of one's waking hours to be dedicated to office time.

Surprisingly, none of the job options came close to Neeraj's stature. We started to wonder if there was anything suitable for the likes of us. He even began to get creative; he once applied for a lecturer's position at a software institute, but the interview process was so mediocre, showing a complete lack of respect from the institute, that he changed his mind.

Job Interview

One evening, Neeraj returned after an interview, and I opened the door with a smile. "How was it?"

Neeraj had a subtle smile on his face. Guessing that maybe the interview hadn't gone well, I kept quiet and offered him a glass of water.

"It was okay." He shrugged.

"Was it not to your expectations?" I ventured.

Slowly sipping from his glass, he replied, "Who says so? The interview was terrific. They were pleased with my level of expertise, exposure, and experience in the field." Glancing at my puzzled expression, he continued, "I was also happy with the vetting process."

"So, you didn't like the company or the setup?" Somehow, I knew that face when I saw it, and I certainly did not see the excited expression had the outcome been favorable.

Briefly looking at the ceiling, Neeraj answered, "I loved the position they offered, manager on an overall interface they are trying to build with the American client. I am very comfortable with their technology and the software platform, and there is a likelihood of getting to work on new emerging software. I also see the potential for growth in my role."

He painted a rosy and hopeful picture. It certainly was a bit of good news after five months, but remembering his expression when he entered the house, I asked, "Then why the face? What are you not telling me?"

"Well, this golden opportunity comes with a catch: until the project ends, I would always be at the client site in the U.S." He began laughing.

My "why?" pout turned into a "whatever" expression, and, frowning at Neeraj, I said, "Just forget it."

As soon as employers learned that you were an American citizen, they wanted to send you back to America where they could bank on your experience and perhaps save their firm any further visa processing. It would also save them time and investment in grooming new employees. However, they failed to understand that we had returned specifically so we could live and work in India, and we did not need their help to get to the U.S., which we could do anytime.

"Well, that's what I was talking about before our move," Neeraj answered, smiling with an I-told-you-so expression.

After a few similar interviews, we concluded that we certainly needed jobs, but not at the cost of staying apart. Yet the opportunities that came our way tested our patience, as they mostly involved traveling to or settling in America or Europe.

That was also when we realized that resettling in India was going to require more effort and dedication than we'd anticipated. I felt we had underestimated the challenges of running a household in contemporary India. We had planned everything based on our knowledge of a First-World Country. For instance, within the first or second month in America, I would have properly set up my entire house, let alone an apartment. But even after a whole year in our Mumbai apartment, not even half the size of my house in Colorado, we were still struggling to line up carpenters and household help.

Moreover, I was busy with parental responsibilities. Not knowing what to expect, I was always on my toes, keeping an eye on Ronak's school and wondering whether we should keep him there. At the same time, I was overwhelmed by mastering how best to interact with the maids, hiring and firing them, setting their schedules, and hiring cooks and others. Sometimes, it felt like I was learning an entirely different skill set unrelated to my software skills, and my job began to resemble something more like that of a personnel manager, a quality-control supervisor, and a psychological counselor—three jobs rolled into one. As a mother, you constantly switch between multiple roles, but the ones I assumed now depended on what was needed to keep our household running smoothly, in addition to the role of a parent.

So, in light of all this and to be with Ronak every step of the way in a new country of residence, I decided that I would not work in our initial years in India.

Someone Like Us Works Here?

One evening, Neeraj and I sat on our balcony sipping tea after I had returned from a birthday party with Ronak. Watching the sunset descend through shades of pink and orange before melting into gray while we listened to the noisy, happy children running around the garden as they brought the whole place alive was bliss. As we relaxed, I casually mentioned a new acquaintance I had met at the sports club party.

"One of the mothers I met at the party said they were nonresident Indians too. I never saw her at our sports club before today.

They came back after six years in Australia. It felt good to meet other NRIs who returned to the motherland with the whole family." It was rare to meet someone with a journey so similar to ours. "But, unlike us, they moved here with his job," I continued. "Naveena's husband worked at a multinational company and transferred here from Australia."

Neeraj looked intrigued. "Oh, so he works on-site for a company in Mumbai?"

Excited, I answered in one breath. "Yes, he works a nine-to-five job in Mumbai. I'm meeting Naveena tomorrow so I can find out more about their work experience in India."

Neeraj nodded. "It's good that we know at least one person who works in Mumbai after experiencing the work environment abroad."

"But we already know one," I countered. "Remember Rakesh, my old friend who gave us some tips and information before he moved to India? I phoned him about five months ago to see how he was doing in India. He lives in Hyderabad and owns a two-thousand-square-foot, custom-built house that even includes furniture imported from America."

This got Neeraj interested. "Wow! Living the American dream in India!" he said wryly.

"Rakesh interviewed for an India-based company and secured the job before returning to India. He said something interesting: that even though we NRIs want to return here as technical expertise, the companies in India want us to assume jobs in upper management because the technical jobs can be picked up by newcomers or midlevel employees. The reason is the volume of technical people available, as well as the younger generation being hired in the campus interviews at India's top engineering colleges. They are well-versed in technology, are teachable, and grasp things quickly. So, when we come with experience from the U.S., they want us to serve as an interface between the American company and the Indian workforce."

"So what?" Neeraj shrugged, not understanding the point.

"Well, Rakesh now manages two hundred people in Hyderabad, and it's very stressful. He ends up working much more than he expected—no family time, fewer weekends, and constant conferences with the American interface. He's even thinking of going back to America."

"Wow, going back?" Neeraj looked surprised as he sipped his tea.

"Yes. I didn't tell you earlier because you had just begun looking for work, and I didn't want Rakesh's experiences to cloud your judgment."

"And they won't," Neeraj insisted. "Our reasons for returning to India are different, and we are not looking for the same answers as Rakesh was."

I nodded happily, pleased by Neeraj's positive attitude as I sat back and finished my tea, watching the pale pink and gray horizon.

One month later, Mrs. Ramani, an ex-colleague of my mother's, visited us one evening to see my new apartment. We were talking over a cup of tea when she suddenly steered her focus to Neeraj. "So, *beta*, where are you working now?"

We explained that we were still waiting for the right opportunity to come along.

Her face lit up. "Oh, my neighbor's son started working in this IT company as soon as he graduated. I can talk to him if you like." Auntie clearly knew nothing about the IT industry.

"Auntie, it's so hot in here—please come sit under the fan. And would you like a piece of cake?" I tried my level best to change the subject.

"No cake for me. Some Marie biscuits would be enough," she said. "But I am surprised after six months, you people have not found jobs. You should be willing to take any job."

I tried to explain without offending her. "Auntie, we had great jobs with higher pay scales in America, but we left it all behind to move here. Hence, we're looking for better opportunities, meaning suitable job profiles and somewhat equivalent pay scales, not entry-level positions. Still, we are very comfortable with our financial situation and can support ourselves longer."

Undaunted, Auntie, a retired government employee, continued doling out advice. "An individual who remains unemployed in a city like Mumbai can never find anything elsewhere. Why don't you look for a teaching job then?"

Having heard enough, Neeraj politely excused himself and walked out with his phone.

Thankfully, when he returned later, Mrs. Ramani was gone, and I immediately apologized for her presumptuous and unsolicited advice.

"Don't worry; it's not your fault," Neeraj replied. "But I'm amazed at the confidence and ease with which she discussed a subject she knows nothing about."

Not long after, we met for coffee at our sports club's restaurant with Naveena and her husband, Santosh, the Indian couple from Australia. They had arrived around the same time we had, and we discovered that they shared questions and dilemmas similar to ours.

"So, how does it feel to be working in the homeland?" Neeraj asked Santosh.

"Well, it has its challenges," Santosh acknowledged. "The commute is just too strenuous here."

"What do you do?" I asked.

"I work on a customized software application."

I said with a broad smile, "Santosh, welcome to the group. We are information technology professionals too."

Neeraj added, "We're curious to know more about NRI IT professionals' work experiences in Mumbai."

Santosh's eyes lit up. "Okay, so whatever we knew abroad about work hours?" he paused, letting the question hang in midair.

"Yes?" we both replied automatically.

"Well, it isn't like that here," Santosh said. "People still maintain the old ideas of putting all their time into work, even though work hours are 'supposed' to be nine to six. You're expected to be at work from eight forty-five a.m. till seven or seven-thirty p.m., at least on a no-deadline day. When you have a deadline, there is no concept of office hours; you are in all the way."

"What happens if you take the nine-to-six schedule at face value?"

Santosh took a long sip of coffee before continuing. "Well, I always drove to work, but the commute was longer, so I started taking the local train. However, in order to catch my train, I had to leave the office on time. But after one month of leaving the office at six, I began receiving calls from my boss to discuss trivial issues in the office. One day, he even casually asked me over the phone if I was stepping out early."

"I worked in Mumbai fifteen years ago, before I went to America," I offered. "In those days, we had the same issues. Employees were expected to be on time or, preferably, come in early, but getting out of the office was always subject to how the superiors might view it."

"True, I recall similar experiences," Neeraj chimed in. "But after so many years, I hoped things had changed for the better."

After a long pause, Santosh said, "Well! Think again!"

Neeraj mused, "In Denver, we both worked downtown, but within an hour's commute. We got home in time to pick up Ronak from daycare and still had the entire evening for family walks or a badminton game in our backyard."

Naveena sighed longingly. "Back in Australia, we also had predictable schedules and lots of family time at the end of the day."

"It's such a shame that employers don't value employees' family time as much as they emphasize punctuality in office arrival time," I said. Recalling my time in the old Mumbai, I was sorry to see how little things had changed.

21

Ganesh Festival on the Konkan Coast

Ganapati is seated in our village temple for this festival.

"Ganapati Bappa Morya!" The chant filled the ether that monsoon day.

I was fortunate enough to take Ronak to my dad's ancestral home in his village to celebrate the Ganesh Festival in my grandma's presence. My dad's native place, in the Konkan Region, located on the Western Coast of Maharashtra, is the most beautiful, serene, and naturally blessed place on Earth. In September 2010, I found a golden opportunity to travel with Ronak on the snake-like roads over the Sahyadri mountain range to this village, roughly 500 kilometers from Mumbai. Every year, one of the houses around the temple gets the opportunity to host the Ganapati Festival and *puja* in the village temple. It was my family's turn to host the *puja* after twelve years. Everyone from my family—my mom, sister, uncles, and their families, and aunts—would join my grandma in the village. Neeraj couldn't accompany us, as he had a job interview in Pune, so I decided to take Ronak and join our extended family for the festival.

Throughout my childhood, I usually visited Konkan during the hot summer, so I wondered if Ronak would enjoy that September visit, as I would also experience this season in the village for the first time.

But traveling to Konkan that September was a visual treat as we journeyed through the lime-green mountains and tropical vegetation. When we arrived, our village resembled heaven on Earth, with abundant blossoms everywhere following the life-giving monsoon season. The sweet, earthen aroma filled the air and captivated our senses.

In addition to the regular flowers, like hibiscus, lilies, and delicate *aboli*, colorful wild balsam topped the green grass swaying in that soothing September breeze, wrapping everything in a sweet scent. Surrounded by tall green trees, the plentiful rice fields painted the whole universe green. I couldn't take my eyes off those picture-perfect landscapes. The weather, too, was comparatively cooler and pleasant. The sounds of "Ganapati Bappa Morya" welcoming Lord Ganesh punctuated the familiar calm in that place. It was a divine feeling.

The whole of nature came together to welcome and celebrate the arrival of Lord Ganesh—the God of intelligence, who removes all obstacles. We, Hindus, believe he visits Earth for a few days during that festival.

My grandma's home sat between a huge backyard and a giant front yard boasting a *tulsi vrindavan* and two old jackfruit trees guarding the house. She announced with pride that my father had planted those jackfruit trees in his childhood. Seeing them standing tall after so many years was a great joy. I always admired the backyard full of exotic fruit trees, such as mangoes, jackfruits, and *ratambe*, among others. There were also flowers like fragrant gardenia and red hibiscus.

I was ecstatic to see my *gaavchi aaji* (paternal grandmother from the village). Her oval face and brown eyes instantly brightened to see us. Her back had hunched with old age, yet she still wore a nine-yard *saree* in *nauvari* style. Even at eighty, she was a calm and hardworking woman. Like all the grandmas, she was an excellent chef. I loved her traditional Marathi delicacies that had been passed down in our family for generations.

Aaji had readied the house for the celebration and packed the storage room with grains, coconuts, and all the other necessities for the arrival of her entire family—kids, grandkids, and most importantly, her great-grandchild, Ronak. During those magical five days, everyone participated in the preparations, beginning with fetching drinking water from the well, then cutting vegetables, cooking food, making flower arrangements in the temple, and making *rangoli*.

Ronak enjoyed helping with *rangoli* coloring and decorating the temple for Lord Ganesh's arrival.

On the first day of the Ganesh Festival, after the rooster's crowing at dawn, the male members and kids in the house took an early bath. They visited the sculptor's shop to ceremoniously bring home the Ganesh idol, which my grandma and her neighbors had selected about a month prior. Once the men brought the idol into the temple, the female members, who were dressed in colorful *sarees* and traditional jewelry, welcomed Lord Ganesh by offering *diyas*, flowers, water, and goodies. Fresh vegetarian delicacies cooked in our kitchen were offered to the Ganesh idol during all five days of the festival. The nightly Ganesh prayers—*aarti*, with the accompaniment of musical instruments like *taal*, *mridangam*, and harmonium—created an atmosphere that was festive, magical, and holy. It was a very fulfilling experience to worship Lord Ganesh with my extended family in that serene environment.

After the *aarti*, our mealtimes meant everyone sat in the great family room on wicker mats spread over the floor. We feasted on lentil soup, rice, mixed-vegetable stew, and sweet *modaks*—a delicacy. I could see Ronak grinning wider whenever my cousins and uncles started teasing each other. He thoroughly enjoyed our extended family's company, and I know he captured those precious moments and treasured them forever.

On the evening of the fifth day, we bid goodbye to Ganapati Bappa in a lovely procession to the village river with a heartfelt request that he visit us next year. After one more Ganapati prayer on the riverbank, the idol was immersed in the river.

The next day, we all decided to visit Harkul, a village located a few miles south of ours, where Aaji's youngest sister lived with her

family in a small farmhouse. As hardworking farmers, they culti-
vated a field of rice and millet. Traveling in two bullock carts, we
arrived at her place in forty-five minutes. It was a beautiful house on
a hillock with terraced rice fields, where cows and buffaloes sat grazing on dried grass below the shed while chickens wandered freely
in the yard. This *aaji* from Harkul was a simple seventy-year-old
woman with a genial smile and curious eyes.

We arrived to find her playing a card game with her grandkids.
Dressed in a *saree* with a mismatched blouse and messy hair, she
looked a bit shocked to see twelve of us on her doorstep unan-
nounced. Certainly, she was unprepared. That's how most visits
occur in villages with no landline phones and very few cell phones.
But she soon wiped the surprise off her face and welcomed us
warmly with questions commonly asked in our villages: "When did
you arrive from Mumbai? And when are you leaving for Mumbai?"
She wanted to know when we were going home because, I remembered from my childhood, she always sent us back with abundant
gifts—jackfruits, homemade coconut sweets, mango sweets, roasted
cashews, and small pouches of rice and powdered horse gram from
their fields.

Being a farmer's family, they were always prepared and had the
summer fruits preserved and the grains in storage. She was incredibly excited to welcome a young American member of our family,
and Ronak was just as ecstatic to meet this new extended family
he had never seen before. But more than that, petting all the cows,
buffaloes, and cats brought a wider smile and pure joy to his animal
lover's heart.

I was so glad I could share with him that happy place from
my childhood memories. Everyone was part of the whole family

celebration and enjoyed it together, further cementing our deep family ties that extended across generations. I realized it was a blessing to relive my childhood memories with Aaji while creating new memories with my son.

A Konkan village house surrounded by tall fruit trees.

☙

22

Our Own Software Company

As mentioned earlier, during our first year in India, I chose not to work outside the home and instead, focused my attention on Ronak. He was overwhelmed with the challenges of moving to an overcrowded city, new and unnecessary norms, a new language, and a new school. My psychology degree, not to mention my mother's intuition, would never allow me to sit still while my child struggled. My goal was to guide him every step of the way while he adjusted to this new life. I even enjoyed being a homemaker and stay-at-home mom during that first year and a half.

But while I stayed home with Ronak, Neeraj struggled to find a job that both fulfilled our needs and did justice to his skills and experience. His expertise was in the oil and gas industry with an emphasis on business functionality rather than just technical knowledge. But the Indian software companies where he interviewed offered no such opportunities.

Neeraj's higher-level technical expertise was not valued much because many younger people with experience in cutting-edge technology were abundantly available and could be hired at a much cheaper rate. That would leave Neeraj with a project management job, managing human resources, but he preferred working on software applications.

He initially thought his expertise could be an asset to the larger Indian company teams. By explaining the business functionality behind the code to the technical teams, he could help them minimize the turnaround time in their performance and reduce software bugs.

But the employers would explain that they already had a project manager on-site at the client's location abroad who took the work requirements from a subject matter expert—an American or European point of contact—and shipped the requirements back to India. The project manager worked at the client site during the day to keep the project running effectively, and to support and manage his Indian team, he would join team meetings over the phone at night, thus remaining on call almost 24/7. That's why the companies Neeraj interviewed with wanted him to go to the U.S. to assume this position—because of his expertise, experience, and citizenship status. However, being American citizens, we did not need work visa sponsorship from anyone.

After hearing other NRIs' experiences, we started seriously considering our work scenario, as we weren't finding the answers we needed. At the same time, we had seen people in the same situation choose different paths, producing different results.

So, in 2010, Neeraj decided to accept an independent consulting opportunity in America instead of returning to work in America as an employee of an Indian company. With troubled hearts, we all agreed. The new position would mean a steady income and offer competitive remuneration to us after nine months of not working. Once Neeraj was back in the U.S. working on the new project, he fortunately found a few additional opportunities for offshore work, which inspired us to set up our own software consulting company in India.

This situation offered the ideal balance and the best of all worlds: I could work for our company from the comfort of home while prioritizing Ronak's school schedule. I could oversee his progress, avoid working-mom guilt, and organize the remaining work on our apartment, thereby keeping our household fully functional while Neeraj was in the States. As a working mother, finding that balance was very important to me.

And so, in December 2010, Neeraj and I became equal partners, both company directors of a private limited company. Our firm would hire technical resources as contractors to work on new assignments that came our way from American clientele. Of course, to support U.S. time, we would have to work night hours due to the time difference between the U.S. and India.

Once we hired the contractors, I was free to choose my own hours; most importantly, I could work after the household help had left for the day. I still recall those early days and the minimal setup I arranged on my table: a Vonage phone for overseas calls, a laptop and printer, a few box binders, and an Airtel phone for monitoring my technical team situated in remote locations in India. By our company's second year, I had started working on the software application because, by then, Ronak was in seventh grade and better adjusted to his new life.

I loved it. It felt so uplifting and invigorating to work for my own company, on my own schedule, at my own pace, and at any time of the day or night. I could even work in my pajamas if I wanted. (Thankfully, videoconferencing was not yet an option!)

Meanwhile, Neeraj added new contract terms with his client so he could fly home every other month and work alternate months from India. He found it grueling to fly internationally every month, but he was determined and diligently found a solution to keep our family together.

After 2014, he reduced his hourly rate so he could work from India and travel once or twice every year; of course, the work hours were night hours. I found his gesture extremely compassionate. Thanks to Neeraj's hard work and persistence, we could work from India and maintain a decent income. He was happy he could visit his parents twice a year for two weeks and work from Bengaluru. Sometimes, his parents stayed with us for a month or two in Mumbai. And the work-from-home opportunity allowed him to spend more time with Ronak after he got home from school. In fact, Neeraj described it as a win-win, a flexible situation that allowed him to spend more time with us while working on the technology and projects he loved.

Because Neeraj had to work during the night, it was imperative that he slept during the day. However, sometimes he lost sleep with so many disruptions like doorbells, phones, visitors, and maids who never understood why he worked at night. But later, he realized the importance of a balance between work and health and recognized that sacrificing sleep due to work was not helpful. So, in 2016, we rented an apartment opposite ours as office space, where he could at least count on sleep during afternoons without disturbance and then work from seven p.m. till three a.m.

My win was that at a time when working from home was still a foreign concept in India, I could work from home and invest my time in our company while also tending to my family.

An American VP in a Multinational Company

I was at a friend's birthday party when she introduced me to a middle-aged man named Aarav. He was her childhood friend and spoke with an American accent. I learned that he had lived in Mumbai for a year and had been transferred from a multinational company in Arizona to a senior position, which piqued my curiosity.

I mentioned our American citizenship status to him, and we instantly clicked. We talked about our experiences in Mumbai. He shared that his family found it tricky living in India. Aarav's expression grew serious when I asked about his personal experience working in India. After a short pause, he rolled his eyes. "It's a nightmare," he confided. "There is a drastic difference between what people say and what they do."

"Oh . . . meaning?" I probed carefully.

"You must watch your back all the time in the office, not knowing when someone will try to drag you down." He sighed. "I'm tired of watching my back. Just yesterday, I had such a challenging day at work because of this backstabbing competitiveness. It's tough."

"Oh, my. I knew it would be challenging but had no idea it was that bad," I offered sympathetically.

Perhaps hoping to change the subject, Aarav quickly asked, "So, what do you do?"

"My husband and I own our own software company," I replied. "I feel lucky that we work from home for our American clientele."

I was surprised when I received a call from Aarav five days later, hoping to clarify his comments. "You caught me off guard that day," he explained. "It was a bad day. And in my bad mood, I spoke out of turn. Let's talk it over some time. Really, working in India is not all that bad."

I understood he was hoping to downplay his earlier comments, but I had heard as much as I needed to. This conversation only solidified my certainty that, although Neeraj and I had done many things on a whim, we had done this one wise thing: start our own company, choosing to work alongside a known clientele. We were accustomed to working with that clientele, and therefore, did not have to adjust to that territory.

23

Unlearn American Ways?

As we settled in and adjusted to our new life in Mumbai, some small doubts and concerns began to creep in. We had moved only after carefully considering the support of my immediate and extended family, who had encouraged the move. But after a few months of living in our apartment, I realized that life in Mumbai was busy, chaotic, and unpredictable, with the doorbell and phone vying for my attention at all hours of the day. I understood that even my loved ones might encounter the same challenges and would find it difficult to share their time and give us their attention, so I adjusted my expectations after our first few months of living in Orion Elevations.

We had intentionally invested in a brand-new apartment complex, created by a top-level builder. But, being an exclusive neighborhood, this affluent community was situated in a way that made it unapproachable for vegetable and fruit vendors and grocery shops. So, we, the residents, had to travel some distance to find those options using some mode of transportation. Meanwhile, my relatives living in their established old neighborhoods had easy access to all those services.

I often missed the convenience of my American neighborhood, where everything I might need—grocery store, restaurant, home goods or decor—was no more than a ten-minute drive away. In my later years in Mumbai, I was pleased to find that it took only a short phone call to small vendors located in those old neighborhoods, and they would deliver groceries and produce as long as you ordered a lot from them and possibly offered a hefty tip to the delivery person.

Managing the daily household chores, even with paid help, remained a frustrating and time-consuming challenge in our new home, much more so than it had been in Denver. In the U.S., we strategized our time. When you knew that you had to complete household tasks with machines, you planned them well. There, the chores and calling the maid got done at our convenience, on our schedule, so we could enjoy "me time" and family time, which were luxuries in Mumbai. I often waited endlessly for maids or deliveries to appear, only for them to arrive late.

Around 2015, as internet marketing took hold and rejuvenated the Indian market, prepaid deliveries of groceries and fresh produce became available from supermarket chains and a few dot-coms. However, in my experience, despite an agreed-upon delivery window, they would invariably arrive at the most inconvenient times. But I was aware that I was looking at those issues from a different lens, based on time already spent in America. I knew I had to open my heart to the new India.

Ye Kaha Aa Gaye Hum?

I was perplexed by this contrast between East and West and challenged by the changes to our lifestyle as we transitioned from house to apartment. While the festive public celebrations in Mumbai amazed us, the overpopulated city overwhelmed us. Also, compared to America, life in Mumbai required far more daily human interactions, to which we slowly adapted.

Even simply crossing the street was fraught with danger. At times, if I wanted to cross a main road, I often found myself stuck and terrified, unable to step into this never-ending stream of oncoming cars, autorickshaws, and bikes that rarely stopped at a traffic light unless the police were present. It was disheartening to witness the relentlessly pushy nature of the crowds at stores and on the roads and also the unnecessarily speeding traffic. Feeling both confounded by how to respond to these situations and puzzled by the challenges of managing my time around the house, I became consumed by one question: *What am I doing here?* Or, to sum it up in Hindi, *Ye kaha aa gaye hum?*

Which led to the next most obvious question: *Why am I here?*

My relatives were here.

My culture was here.

The food I loved was available in abundance.

Even if I hadn't found the ideal household help, at least help was available.

But still, questions remained.

After Neeraj began traveling again to the U.S., we meticulously planned our family vacations around his schedule and Ronak's summer breaks, so Ronak could see India beyond Mumbai and enjoy family time. On a trip to Rajasthan in 2011, we met a family from Hyderabad. Because our kids had similar interests in photography and wildlife, we, moms, connected well. While traveling in the hotel's sightseeing minibus, she mentioned that her family had moved from the U.S. East Coast. I was excited that after two years in India, I had finally found someone from whom I could get tips and advice.

"So, how long has it been since you moved to India?" I asked, like a fish gulping for air when outside the water.

"Seven years," she answered nonchalantly.

Hearing her casual reply, I hesitated to ask more. *What if it's just us who are struggling?* However, I finally asked, "So . . . you had no issues adjusting to life back in India?"

"Believe me, we had our share of adjustments after we moved." Shifting her gaze from the window to me, she smiled reassuringly. "It takes a solid five years to adjust in India, especially coming from America." When I pressed further, she said, "Don't dismiss what you're going through as nothing just because people around you don't understand and interpret it like you do."

Instantly, I felt a rush of relief. Her wisdom and advice released me from the discomfort I'd been feeling, a vague sense of disappointment that our adjustment wasn't going well. So many people around us hadn't understood our challenge. "If you were born here, then how do you not remember these things?" one of my relatives had asked me the first year after the move. "This is how it is. You don't question it," another had rebuked.

But most of them had not seen the American side of our lives, so they had no frame of reference for what we were going through, the adjustments we had to make, especially relearning Indian ways, while also unlearning our American life habits. Thanks to the kind words of my fellow traveler, I was prepared to be kinder to myself.

CR

24

Courtesy and Patience
in Modern Mumbai?

When I was growing up in India, my parents deeply ingrained in me the principles of courtesy and social etiquette. After moving to the States, I experienced remarkable courtesy and awareness of respecting others' dignity in suburban Colorado. I expected the same once I returned to India, but even though everything felt new and changed, there were a few social etiquette habits and norms that continued to annoy us. It's important to point out, however, that I grew up in a middle-class environment with middle-class values, but when I returned to India, it was to an upper-middle-class society. So, perhaps this difference accounts for some of the issues.

I remember two particular topics revolving around issues of courtesy that left us speechless.

Staring

It was hard not to be taken aback by this issue. After completing our aqua fitness session in the swimming pool, one of my class buddies, Sangita, and I chatted as we walked toward the shower rooms. I noticed a tall, hefty man across the pool, standing on the edge of the pool in his swimming trunks, staring at us. His stare was so incessant that I thought he might be Sangita's husband or boyfriend. Why else would he be peering at us so obviously? I certainly didn't recognize him or remember ever seeing him before.

When we reached the corner of the swimming pool where he stood, I waited for Sangita to acknowledge or greet him, but instead, she walked right by. Meanwhile, he continued to gawk at us without blinking. I was dumbfounded.

"Don't you know him?" I asked Sangita.

"Me, why?" She shrugged. "I've never seen him before."

"Then why has he been staring at us nonstop for the last three minutes?" I asked, incredulously.

"It's okay. You have to learn to accept it; men always stare at women. It's part and parcel of living here," she said.

I was utterly mystified. "I understand it happening when we walk down the street," I countered, "but at our sports club, I expect educated club members to exhibit good manners. At least here, we should be able to hold people accountable for these behaviors."

"It's just what happens here; some men stare like that. There's nothing we can do." Sangita sounded as if she had given up.

"Well, even if we can't do anything to change their behavior, at least we can protest in our own way," I snarled, unable to contain myself.

Suddenly, I remembered my mother's favorite saying growing up: "If you step on an ant, the ant bites back too." *Why should an educated human being let this kind of behavior slide? We should complain*, I thought. In Mumbai, I realized some elements of society, irrespective of their age, gender, or class, either knowingly or unknowingly feel it's okay to ogle a person. The basic concept of rude behavior might not even occur to them.

Growing up in Mumbai, I had learned how to safeguard myself despite the obnoxious staring habit of some individuals. But I'd forgotten all about these uncomfortable gazes during my decade and a half in Colorado. After our return to India, I didn't know how to handle these stares; they made me feel self-conscious and cautious, pushing me to be on my toes and always watching my back. At least the staring habit was not widespread; only certain people engaged in it. But I had met numerous women, just like my swimming buddy, who weren't affected by someone staring at them. They led their lives as though being stared at was part and parcel of every woman's life.

One morning at our sports club, I had purposely chosen to take my morning walk a little later than usual, hoping to avoid the regular crowd and have the track to myself. I found two people walking the track—a middle-aged woman in a tracksuit, and a man in his early twenties. The young man minded his own business, but the woman stared at me while I completed my warm-up stretches. Even though, other than the young man, the entire five-hundred-meter track was empty, the woman would invariably scrutinize my every move each time she walked by. I guessed that she came from a well-off family, based on her clothes and demeanor. Perhaps her gaze was not as annoying as that of the man at the swimming pool. Nevertheless, staring was rude, and it made me uncomfortable.

In fact, the more she stared, the more self-conscious, and, eventually, irritated, I became. So, I decided to stare back at her. What followed was a rather amusing experience; I was a little uncomfortable doing this, but to my surprise, she slowly realized after three long, relentless stares from me, and became self-conscious. Unsure how to react, she first smiled at me and then stopped looking my way the rest of the time she was present on the track. This finally allowed me to complete my workout in peace.

Hold the Door, Please . . .

We were also troubled by people's etiquette when it came to holding doors for others. One Sunday afternoon, we visited an iconic hotel's buffet restaurant. The place was jam-packed with patrons coming in for lunch, while others exited after their sumptuous brunch. The hotel seemed very busy with the weekenders in addition to a wedding celebration in progress. After lunch, engrossed in our conversation, Neeraj, Ronak, and I left the restaurant; we were followed by a small crowd exiting behind us.

Neeraj held the door for Ronak and me as we stepped outside the restaurant, but Neeraj could not pass through the door, as the people behind us nonchalantly started pushing past. Not one or two but ten people, at least, appeared utterly oblivious that someone was holding the door for them. They went on about their business without acknowledging, let alone appreciating, that Neeraj was still holding the door.

Ronak and I watched as Neeraj inadvertently served as door attendant for this stampede of strangers. As he patiently accommodated them, Ronak, amused by this scenario, walked toward Neeraj and asked, "Dad, why are these people not even thanking you? Maybe they think you're a doorman?"

At last, the restaurant manager appeared and took charge of the door, allowing Neeraj to join us. The manager thanked him, to which Neeraj replied casually, "It's okay." Neeraj scratched his chin and contemplated for a second, then asked Ronak, "Why did you think those people thought I was a doorman?"

"Because in our apartment building, I've seen a few residents ask the security guard to hold the door for them," Ronak explained enthusiastically. "They also expect him always to greet them as 'Sir.'"

"Really! The guard has to hold the door for everyone?" Neeraj frowned.

"Yes," I chimed in. "It's hard to believe, but it's true. Certain people expect it from the guard."

"But those residents only notice the guard if he forgets or delays in greeting them," Ronak added.

"Well, if it is true, that is just plain rude." Neeraj shook his head in frustration. "Back in Colorado, people always held doors for others, and particularly elevator doors, to let others get on comfortably. Even the CEOs of our companies held the door for the employees."

"Yes. To you and me, and a few others trying to do the right thing, it's rude, but I doubt if those people in the restaurant today even realized the rudeness of their behavior."

Sadly, experiences like this were not uncommon. I worried that common decent courtesy was slowly disappearing in this overpopulated, fast-paced city. I also worried that the more you came across as humble, the faster you got shot down. Perhaps certain aspects of courtesy had already vanished in some bigger American cities, but we always compared everything to Denver.

With a nod of regret, I realized it was up to me to change my expectations so I might adjust better to the new Mumbai. As that mother from Hyderabad had advised, it would take five full years for us to acclimate enough to ignore these irritations.

C3

25

Our Mode of Transportation

Ronak gradually adjusted to his new Indian school and graduated from fifth grade with flying colors. His school had finally moved to its newly constructed building in Malad, a fifteen-minute drive from our home. However, Neeraj and I weren't yet comfortable with sending Ronak to and from school on the unreliable school buses. We didn't entirely trust the unskilled drivers and unacceptable conditions of those subcontracted buses. We'd read stories in the newspapers about students being injured after falling out of school buses because the drivers were in a rush and didn't allow children sufficient time to get on and off.

Besides, in Denver, we'd always had to take Ronak to and from his charter school, so we gladly assumed that responsibility in Mumbai as well. Ronak, of course, was not too happy with the idea of riding to school with Mom or Dad. And since we weren't sure how long we'd stay in India, we hadn't yet bought a car. So, we relied on the other modes of transportation.

I quickly realized that the bus journey was not my cup of tea anymore. Cabs were not easy to find in the suburbs unless you booked them in advance, and a bicycle was impractical. That left me with only one option—autorickshaws.

Autorickshaws were widely available in the suburbs, and considering their agility in negotiating narrow lanes with ease, they were our preferred choice for a regular commute. Still, the everyday routine of trying to spot a rickshaw and then convincing the driver to take us to our destination proved to be an exercise in patience and frustration. Before long, it became clear that even the autorickshaw option was not going to work long-term.

Even though Ronak's school was only fifteen minutes away, we had to leave the house forty-five minutes before school started so we'd make it on time. Our newly built neighborhood was away from the main roads, so no autorickshaws or cabs waited at the entrance. Plus, there were no bus stops close by, so we had to walk till we found a rickshaw.

Taking Ronak to his evening art class around five p.m. was especially difficult, as we competed with the office crowd pouring into the streets. They hired most of the autorickshaws before the vehicles reached us, and the ones available for hire just passed by, ignoring customers. We would wave and stop them, but they were not interested in going such a short distance. The drivers would give all sorts of excuses, such as, "I want to go straight," or, "Your destination is in the opposite direction for me." And you couldn't argue with them.

We managed a rickshaw commute for two academic years, but by then, I'd had enough, especially while Neeraj was away working in the U.S.

I told Neeraj one day over the phone, "A car is the best solution to escape overcrowded buses, inconvenient bus stop locations, and forever unwilling and unavailable autorickshaw drivers. Once we have a car, I can take Ronak to school peacefully in the mornings." In my mind, though, I was thinking, *It's ridiculous that we need to buy a car just to drive Ronak to and from school.*

Back in America, I had been certain we'd never need a car in Mumbai. Because old Mumbai's public transportation had been so good, I had assumed I would easily be able to hail cabs or autorickshaws. When I was growing up in India, cars were considered a luxury, and we never owned one. So, I assumed Neeraj, Ronak, and I could manage without a car after our move. But after we moved to India, we realized cars were not uncommon; some of our neighbors had two cars per household. Yet we had never thought about buying a car until now.

"I knew it then." Neeraj was ready with his in-depth analysis. "Even when you said we wouldn't need cars in India, I questioned your words. After living in America for so long, we got spoiled by the comforts of our cars. I don't know why you thought we'd be content with using cabs or buses in India. Besides, times have changed. Things are not the same as when we were young and working in India."

"I guess I still lived in that time capsule and thought India would not have changed so fast and that commuting on public transportation would not be so taxing on my time and physical comforts," I admitted. "But who would have imagined hailing a cab or autorickshaw would be so complicated?" I thought about the SUVs, minivans, and sedans we'd owned over the years in America and said, "I miss my Honda and Toyota, and I guess I'll still miss them in India."

"Why?" Neeraj sounded surprised. "Aren't you buying a new car?"

"Yes, but I won't be driving it—the chauffeur will," I replied, excited.

"Why a chauffeur? You've been driving for thirteen years in Denver."

"Are you kidding?" I scoffed. "The autorickshaw drivers drive like there's no tomorrow, and the motorbikers are even worse."

"So what?" Neeraj sounded unaffected. "You know better than that!"

"No, Neeraj, it's very unsafe driving in the city." My concern was genuine. "Some people don't follow any traffic rules. Some drivers have a rat-race mentality. They just want to get ahead by using the shortcuts, even if it means that others will have to wait or are put in danger because of it."

Neeraj quickly replied, "Take lessons if you feel it's difficult driving in India. Maybe you're not comfortable driving on the left side of the road."

A little peeved by his suggestion, I countered, "Driving lessons? I've been driving for thirteen years; I don't need training." After a pause, I continued, "However, I do need practice driving on Mumbai's busy, crowded streets." I reluctantly acknowledged the need for lessons, regardless of my proficiency in driving.

So, we decided over the phone that I would buy a car once I got my Indian driver's license. Without a vehicle, I thought the driving school was the best option to practice for the driver's license test, as they provided a car for the lessons.

The front desk at the driving school informed me that after two weeks of classes, I could appear for a driving test at the Regional Transport Office (RTO). So, I registered for the lessons.

My Car Research

I had learned to drive in America, so I was only familiar and comfortable with driving a left-hand-drive vehicle on the right-hand side of the road. And I'd driven only cars with automatic transmissions. So, it was a given that I would drive an automatic car. But I hadn't realized that in India, there wasn't much demand for automatic transmissions in those days.

While researching cars with automatic transmissions, one day, I summoned a Honda salesman for a test drive around my area—but it wasn't that simple. The driver's seat was on the right, and the car had to be driven on the left side of the road—precisely the opposite of the setup in the U.S. So, there began my struggle as I sat in the driver's seat, depressed the accelerator, and impulsively aimed for the right side of the road. The car dealer sitting next to me frowned and quickly guided me to the left side of the road. Once on the left, I drove well on the less-busy backroads of our community, but when I gauged the size of the Honda Civic compared with the streets and lanes near Ronak's school, Malad, and Goregaon, my stomach lurched. Driving in the Mumbai suburbs meant maneuvering in narrow lanes and on roads with no lane markings or dividers. You had to take sharp turns without hitting a bicyclist, motorcyclist, or autorickshaw driver.

I needed a smaller car for narrow roads, yet an automatic transmission remained a priority. Sadly, at the time, neither Honda nor Toyota had any smaller-size automatic transmission cars besides the Civic and Avalon models. So, feeling discouraged, I had to expand my search beyond these two manufacturers. I started with the famous Maruti Suzuki. This company offered several smaller-size cars, but none were automatic. People told me it would be impossible to find a small car with an automatic transmission. As disconcerted as I was, I never gave up.

"Just buy a Honda Civic," Neeraj advised over the phone. "You have plenty of experience driving one, and you'll feel comfortable in it." He worried that car buying was becoming time-consuming.

"No, I don't think that will work," I said. "People do drive bigger cars here, but looking at the vehicles huddled together with no lane markings on the roads, I feel uncomfortable. I want a car small enough to move easily in and out of tight spaces."

At last, I was relieved to learn that Hyundai manufactured a small hatchback with an automatic transmission. Visiting the dealer showroom, I found a very compact car. When this beauty ran on the roads of Mumbai, it could effortlessly maneuver through traffic jams and small, tight lanes. However, since most drivers preferred the stick-shift option, I had to load up my car with premium features and spend an extra Rs 400,000 for the automatic transmission, which was absurd! Astonishingly, after buying the top-of-the-line model, I still had to wait two months to have the car delivered.

But finally, after two years of rickshaw commuting, I had my automatic compact ride—a Hyundai i10 Next Generation—in ruby red. Ronak had helped me choose the color. In the meantime, I continued my practice sessions at the driving school.

ભ

26

Driving! Only for a Braveheart

"*Bumbai main car chalaana hai to ghoose jaavo, log apne aap side me hutenge,*" my driving instructor preached to me on a narrow, crowded lane in one of Mumbai's Western suburbs on a weekday morning.

The scene was utter chaos with pedestrians, hawkers, cars, bikes, and autorickshaws battling for both space and forward motion. I was reluctant to speed up, fearing I might hit a pedestrian. While I faced this dilemma, cars coming from the opposite direction took advantage, speeding up and encroaching on my driving space, virtually pushing my car off the tar road. But if I dared to release the brake, motorbikes in the lane behind me started honking, impatient to pass, which only increased my rising anxiety. In thirteen years of driving in America, I'd probably been honked at only three or four times. Honking was considered rude in Colorado, but in Mumbai, you risked being honked at even while walking along the road minding your own business.

"Step on the pedal and move ahead fearlessly," my instructor repeated firmly. "That's how to make the pedestrians and other cars make way for your car."

"Okay, but why do the bikers keep honking?" I asked edgily.

"They're just warning you that they are quickly passing on the left side of your car," he answered casually. It was no big deal—to him.

Great! So, it's not my fault. I was relieved. Here I was, overanalyzing my driving and finding flaws because of their rude behavior while, for my instructor and the other drivers, honking was merely business as usual.

Driving had been such a pleasant experience in Colorado, primarily because of the state's breathtaking scenic views. Undoubtedly, well-maintained roads and neatly drawn lane markers contributed to the ease of gliding through the mountains. Even on the interstate highway, driving seventy-five miles per hour, the gorgeous landscape remained always in view, thanks to fewer distractions and less commotion on the road. The majority of drivers followed the rules, stayed in their respective lanes, and switched lanes only when safe and after clearly signaling their intentions. The DMV (Department of Motor Vehicles) guidelines were clear for each driver taking a license test: "defensive driving." In the United States, I remember living by the underlying principle of "better safe than sorry" when it came to driving.

When I originally signed up for driving lessons in Mumbai, it was because I needed practice with left-side driving and driving on busy roads. But when the instructor arrived with a stick-shift car, my heart sank. So, now, I had to add learning to drive a stick shift car to my list. And so, there I was, listening to my instructor's great advice in the middle of the crowded street as I struggled to drive that manual transmission car. Of course, I had signed up for lessons specifically to learn how to handle Mumbai's overcrowded streets, but this instructor was telling me to just step on the pedal and move ahead. "Whatever the outcome, we'll deal with it later"—I hadn't anticipated this type of suggestion when I'd signed up for the lessons! So much for my thirteen years of driving experience and taking the utmost care to be a safe and defensive driver. All my knowledge of road safety was tossed out the window in that crowded, narrow Mumbai lane as my instructor basically undermined all my prior experience and better judgment by telling me to be an "offensive" rather than defensive driver.

Unwilling to move my foot from the brake, I stared at the mad rush of vehicles before me and asked the instructor, "If I step on the gas, how can I be sure that the oncoming traffic will behave and stay on their side of the road?"

Seemingly perplexed by my inhibition, he just looked at me for a moment. "Madam! You decide. Are you worried about the pedestrians or the other cars?"

"Huh?!" I was confused by his priorities.

"We are focused on the pedestrians at present, Madam." He sounded more bored than annoyed.

Needless to say, I ignored his advice and maintained my commitment to driving defensively. Eventually, I gained the confidence to drive assertively in Mumbai's overcrowded streets, and after just five more lessons, I was all set to get my Mumbai license. However, for my peace of mind, I realized I would have to overlook the fact that because of my defensive driving, almost everyone on the road—autorickshaws, buses, small delivery trucks, other sedans, SUVs, or bikes—took advantage by overtaking my car. They misunderstood my courtesy and, regardless of their position on the road, granted themselves right-of-way over my vehicle.

My driving test was scheduled with the city transportation authority (RTO) at the end of the month. I had hoped to get a manual or booklet explaining traffic dos and don'ts, but I never received anything throughout my five lessons. When I requested a manual from my driving school, they placed a single back-to-back-printed sheet in my hand, showing pictures and explanations, such as arrow signs and stop signs. I was more relieved than surprised that there were only two pages of images I needed to memorize for my written test.

Obtaining my driver's license in the U.S. had been much more comprehensive. I recall the DMV handing me a booklet about thirty pages long, including lengthy, descriptive rules about right of way, keeping adequate distance between two vehicles, and much more. Everyone also had to take a thirty-minute written test based on that guidebook, and only after passing the written test could you take the driving test to be eligible for a driver's license in Colorado.

Now in Mumbai, looking at the limited instructions and rules, I wondered about the written test. When I asked at the front desk of the driving school, the receptionist barely looked up from her cell phone as she snapped, "What written test? You will have a driving test on that day." She quickly returned to her screen.

I called the driving school a day before my test and was told I hadn't completed all the lessons, yet the instructor was okay with this—I could have one final session on the way to the test location. I felt relieved to squeeze in one more practice session before getting into test mode at RTO. The following day, when I arrived at the school, I found at least ten more students waiting for the same test. Apparently, each of us had driving tests scheduled for that day, and we would be taken to RTO together. My instructor handed the car keys to me so I could complete my lesson on our way to the transport office.

Okay, I made a note to myself, *this means no more small side roads. You have to drive on busy main roads.* I was a little jittery, as the journey involved driving through heavy traffic. As I started the car, the instructor asked me to wait for the others.

"Others? Who?"

"Some other students taking the test will be coming in our car," he explained.

So, now it looked like I would have an audience for my final driving lesson.

"Wow, it sure sounds like a test to me," I grumbled, venting my real feelings, which, of course, had no effect on the instructor. He waited outside the car until three people lined up to get in our vehicle. I was driving an old Hyundai hatchback, which happened to be stick shift, and as we all knew, would invariably stop at any bump or obstacle in the road while in first gear. With those three fellow students plus one instructor as my audience, I would have to restart the car in the middle of the road without getting worked up, simultaneously turning a deaf ear to the vehicles behind mine, and then calmly continue the drive with those four sets of eyes watching this exercise.

Excellent. By the time we reach RTO, I will certainly be a pro at exercising my patience.

"Okay, let's go." After directing the three students to the back seat, the instructor climbed into the passenger seat.

I started the car, gingerly put it in first gear, checked the rear-view mirror, slowly accelerated, and shifted to second gear, staying focused on the road. The instructor and the others soon grew comfortable and chatty, but I kept my eyes on the road and rearview mirror and focused on being a defensive driver.

Once we reached the transport office, the dilapidated building looked strange. Outside, the waiting area was under a tin shade with some wooden stools arranged as a seating area. Several people were already waiting in different lines; it felt as if we were entering a vast river of people. Each group had its own leader, a representative from their driving school who guided them.

Finally, after two hours of waiting outside on the wooden stools and sweating profusely, we followed our instructor to a computer room in the building. Soon, he disappeared, and we quietly stood in the extensive queue, not knowing what we were in line for. Eventually, upon reaching the front of the line, I realized it was the photo-capturing desk. I wanted to at least look presentable for the license photo, however the reality wasn't so tidy. After spending two hours under the tin shade in the middle of a humid, sunny after-noon, the makeup on my face had dissolved in the deluge of sweat running down my forehead. The officer at the desk didn't even give me enough time to run a comb through my hair as he asked me to verify my address and then snapped the photo immediately. Suddenly, our instructor appeared out of the blue and led us all to where we had started three hours earlier. This time, there were no stools or shade in sight. We had to stand in the middle of the dirt road within the more extensive clay surface. I could see that an artificial intersection had been made, flattening the dirt road, big enough to accommodate four cars on each side of the plus-sign-shaped area. Finally, our instructor appeared in our school's car, accompanied by an officer who would test us on our driving skills.

Curious, I asked the instructor, "Do we have to drive all over this open area?"

"No. The officer will only ask you to drive on this representation of an intersection for forward, reverse, and parallel parking."

Because I'd considered myself an expert at driving in the States, I was slightly disappointed. *So much for my practice sessions in Mumbai, not to mention thirteen years of driving experience in America,* I thought. *It turns out that all I'll be asked to do is drive through this big mock intersection.* But this disappointment was soon superseded by my actual driving test.

We all stood under the sun on this rundown open ground a few meters away from that crossway road. One by one, everyone in the queue would have a chance to get into the car and prove why they deserved a driver's license. However, just a few meters away was a cluster of other students witnessing the test. I observed others undergoing the test before me. Some tests took just two or three minutes, while others took ten minutes, but none lasted longer than that. I told myself that maybe the examiner was not in a good mood, and perhaps he failed those he sent out of the vehicle within a few minutes. Looking at the faces of the students who seemingly flunked, the remaining people in line freaked out and blamed the hot afternoon sun for the officer's mood swings. Slowly, tension mounted. I forgot all about my apprehension about the crowded streets.

On hearing my name called, I approached the car and took the driver's seat while the officer sat in the front passenger seat. I was relieved to see a familiar face—my instructor's— peering at us from the back seat. The officer asked me to verify my information. Hoping to soften his mood, I conversed with him in our native language, Marathi.

When he asked me to restart the car by shutting off the engine and turning the ignition key, I felt relaxed and complied quickly. However, I soon realized the vehicle stood almost in the middle of the makeshift intersection in the dirt road. That spot happened to be bumpy, uneven, and a little elevated. As I moved into first gear and pressed the accelerator right before switching into second, the car stopped, just as it always did during our practice sessions. Only now, it was happening before the officer's eyes, and I couldn't make excuses. So, I stopped the car, restarted, put it in first gear, accelerated a little forcefully, and moved it into second. Eventually, he asked me to reverse the car along the plus sign's edges and parallel park on the dirt road.

At the end of the test, the officer asked me in Marathi how I could have let the car stop. My instructor swiftly jumped to my rescue and explained that the car was ancient and the regular institute car had been unavailable that day. He assured the officer that my driving skills were top-notch. As the officer skimmed his paperwork, suspense built about whether I had passed the test. Finally, he flashed a subtle smile from the corners of his lips, and I exhaled in relief—*I got my Indian license!*

ॐ

27

Tossing My "Hem's List"

I had arrived in India with my extensive "Hem's List" in hand, carefully delineating my hopes, dreams, and expectations for our new life in Mumbai. But once on the ground, I quickly realized that most of the items on my list, far from being absolute necessities, required much more give-and-take. So, with that in mind, I took what I had learned and tore up the list.

People who had lived in India without a break had had the chance to progress with the system gradually over time, so they likely didn't notice or mind these small but regular irritations that we faced so frequently.

Summarizing What I Learned: -

The Corporate Side of Services

The servicepeople who used to perform their duties in the older middle-class communities had been replaced in the tower culture by corporate entities that gave these workers English job titles, such as security guard, maid, chauffeur, and so on. However, the new personnel lacked the necessary training one would expect from people in these roles, and since these workers came from the company, they lacked the motivation and drive of a person hired for the job independently.

Guards: It used to be that a single Nepali Gurkha would guard a building complex, but now, under the new corporate culture, the company sends a team of uniformed guards instead. However, even while dressed in their uniforms and holding their batons, they appear unsure about their responsibilities. Building management had to train them according to the building's needs.

Maids: Before arriving in India, I had dreamt of hiring maids to handle the housework, freeing up my time so I might focus on other projects. But the reality was so different; their irregular schedules and uneven work performance added so much stress to my life that sometimes, I felt I could manage better on my own.

We encountered the same problems with the businesses that ran the maid services. The maids were novices who often lacked skills and experience, and therefore, required your training. But even after you trained them, there was no guarantee they would stick with you; they might be rotated to other houses, leaving you to train their replacements.

Custom furniture: Carpenters rarely arrived on time or followed instructions. Deadlines that had been agreed upon were never met, so custom furniture was, regrettably, rarely worth the effort.

Cars: Even though public transportation is widely available, a car is still necessary, for obvious reasons.

CR

28

My Television Dilemma

"Today's my day, and I'm watching TV as long as I want," Ronak said, enthusiastically declaring his plan for the day. When we woke at six-thirty a.m., it was cloudy and rainy with the dark sky obscuring any daylight. It hadn't stopped pouring since last night, and as I switched on the lamp to find my way out of my bedroom, I questioned whether I should send Ronak to school in that stormy weather.

Stepping carefully across the wet tiles on the balcony, I gauged the weather and was dumbfounded to find that the entire apartment complex was waterlogged. I checked from every balcony in our unit, and it looked the same everywhere. At the edge of the suburb, our building complex stood tall and isolated, without any surrounding clusters of buildings; flooding in suburban Mumbai had generally been caused by overbuilding, but that was not the case here.

I sighed. I remembered the construction company had emphasized that we were safe from flooding here—that was one of the reasons we'd invested in this property. And yet, despite its premium location, our apartment complex now had a substantial amount of water on the ground.

I switched on the TV. In those days, TV and radio news reports were the best sources of updates about the weather in India, and based on that information, parents decided whether to send their children to school. I remembered back in Colorado, we'd had a reliable school closure link on the school's website, which never failed to inform parents about weather-related school closures. Our county helpline had been one more resource for updates during inclement weather. Those resources saved students and their parents from an unnecessary trip to the school in case of a school closure during heavy snow. I dearly missed those helplines through our years in Mumbai.

"The whole Mumbai region continues to receive heavy rains today," the TV newsreader reported. "The Western and Central Mumbai trains are operating only up to Dadar Station." Upsetting film footage showed some of Mumbai's small businesses shut down and underwater. The full scale of this chaos soon became evident. Several regions remained impassable for vehicles, and in some places, cars and autorickshaws were submerged. Suddenly, the amount of water that had accumulated in our complex didn't seem so bad compared with the images on TV. I glanced at Ronak sitting beside me, grinning widely at these images, which meant something very different to him.

"It's just like winter in Colorado," he quipped.

"No, *beta*, this is monsoon season. But it does look hazardous to send you to school."

"What you told me back in Colorado is finally happening? I was wondering when I would get a monsoon day off!"

"Yes, it's your day off," I confirmed.

Ronak was thrilled, and he proclaimed again, "Today is my day, and I am watching TV as long as I want!"

"Ronak, we will do extra Hindi practice today," I explained, hoping not to temper his joy. We negotiated Ronak's TV time, and he agreed to watch for only two hours.

Meanwhile, I kept thinking that in the absence of a school closure website, I had to sit through the news sessions to support my decision—not to send Ronak to school; this took an entire hour of my time.

After our breakfast, Neeraj got busy on his laptop, and I began working on my computer, leaving Ronak sprawled on the sofa with the TV remote control. His interest in the ongoing monsoon news reports was limited, so he channel-surfed, looking for something more entertaining. He landed on a music channel, and I was startled when I heard the lyrics of the first song. I glanced at the screen and saw an actress dancing provocatively to a new Hindi song. Now, I was shocked and appalled, not just by the vulgar words but also by the dress. I knew I had to do something.

"Ronak, you can't watch this! It's not age-appropriate."

He rolled his eyes. "Mom, everybody in my class knows this Bollywood song," he argued. "Just last week, my classmate Saagar was singing it—it's on TV all the time."

Although Ronak generally preferred Cartoon Network or Animal Planet, he persisted in watching the music channel because I had objected to it. So, not knowing how to handle this, I switched the TV back to the news channel.

Neeraj joined us curiously in the living room and nudged me to let Ronak continue watching music videos.

"Really?" I shot back. "You're okay with this? Back in Colorado, I always scrutinized the movie listings for ratings, and when he was younger, we wouldn't even let Ronak watch a Disney movie if it was rated PG-13."

"That's true." Neeraj stroked his chin in thought. "Ronak, you can watch Animal Planet if you want."

Ronak agreed to this reasonable compromise—at least he got his TV time. He was satisfied, but my concern lingered.

"Back in Colorado, we had parental control passwords to restrict certain channels, but here, they don't have that provision. Besides, at this point, I'm not even sure about which channels are to be restricted," I grumbled. "The TV soaps are showing rowdy behavior and are getting more disturbing."

Neeraj nodded. "Yes, I noticed that when I visited my parents and saw some of the soaps my mom watches."

"They have the gall to advertise these shows as family dramas, even though the characters are crazy, psychotic," I continued. "It's dangerous, especially when the whole family, including the kids, are watching." I sat on the couch, fuming, while the monsoon's thunder and lightning mimicked my disgruntled mood.

Neeraj pointed out, "True, but very few find it objectionable."

"Yes, the households with all adult members certainly don't. But as a mother and a psychology student, I understand the risk of kids watching these shows at such an impressionable age," I argued. "Glorifying these deviant behaviors misleads the youth."

During a TV commercial break, Ronak went to the fridge and returned with a snack of watermelon. The next ad promoted a skin-lightening beauty cream, prompting Ronak to ask, "Aai, why do people want to look so fair here?"

My brow furrowed. How best to explain this to my son? "Well, Ronak, people always covet something different from what they have. Here, some women desire lighter-colored skin, while in America, some women use tanning products, especially in summer, hoping to make their skin more tanned."

"Why do they want to show off so much?" Being a preteen boy, Ronak failed to understand the lengths we, women, are willing to go to at times.

While I was talking to Ronak, Neeraj had gone to the kitchen and now returned with a cup of *adrak* chai and some reheated *sabudana vada* from the day before.

"Yum! There is nothing better than a hot ginger chai and deep-fried tapioca patty in the monsoon rain," I said.

When Neeraj offered some to Ronak, he didn't budge; he was now immovable, eyes glued to the TV as he watched some giraffes in the African savanna.

"At least here there aren't so many TV ads for prescription drugs," Neeraj mused, biting into his snack.

I wholeheartedly agreed. "In America, it seemed like there were many ads for a medicine designed to treat weight loss, cancer, or diabetes. I'm glad to see fewer pharmaceutical ads here in India." I sipped my tea and glanced out the window; after the overnight rain, the sky was almost clear, but the tea was still relevant.

⚬⚬

29

Leopards in the City?

As we deepened our roots in Orion Elevations and transformed it into our comfortable residence in Mumbai, we enjoyed many benefits, especially our close proximity to my mom and a few relatives. Still, we always had to face the mind-bogglingly competitive traffic while visiting them.

The Link Road was closer to our apartment complex; several years ago, it had been built over the creek in the Goregaon-Malad area. But now, it had been converted into a major access road connecting the Western suburbs from Bandra to Borivali. It had also become home to many newly constructed, sprawling, upscale neighborhoods, hotels, restaurants, and shopping areas, resulting in an unsurprising increase in heavy traffic, which made us miss Colorado dearly. In Colorado, one Sunday almost every month, we packed our backpacks and either visited Rocky Mountain National Park, drawn in by its mountainous valleys and peaks, or spent the day at the zoo, which was widely spread over a big open space replicating the natural habitats of different types of animals. These trips helped develop Ronak's interest in wildlife and nature. So, when we moved back to India, I was always searching for these captivating natural options within the city to create more desirable reasons for Ronak to stay in Mumbai.

Growing up in Goregaon, we had enjoyed visiting the Aarey Colony vicinity, which featured attractions like an observation point and picnic area. So, hoping Ronak would enjoy Aarey and find more to like about our current city of residence, I took him to visit the park along with my relatives. But I was disheartened to find that the present-day reality did not live up to my rose-tinted memory. Now, the jungle seemed to be shrinking as the ever-expanding city encroached upon the green belt.

Although Ronak had fun to some extent, the area evidently lacked the wilderness feel. Thankfully, he didn't compare it with the gigantic mountains and broader landscapes of Colorado. I realized we might have to wait for another vacation like the one we had taken a year ago to Bandipur National Park to explore the richer Indian wilderness beyond the Mumbai city limits. But Neeraj had returned to the U.S. to work on a project, and taking Ronak on a long trip by myself was out of the question. So, I got creative and looked for options available nearby for the upcoming summer vacation.

Fortunately, we had joined the Bombay Natural History Society (BNHS) a year earlier, to engage Ronak more. The organization's flamingo tours for wildlife enthusiasts had been quite helpful as a fun attraction for him within the city. Thousands of migratory lesser and greater flamingos visit the wetlands of Mumbai's coastline in winter, and observing these long-legged, pink-feathered birds wading in clusters in the water was an awe-inspiring sight.

Flamingos are wintering in the Mumbai creek.

In the summer of 2011, I came across a wilderness overnight camp organized by BNHS for kids ages ten to thirteen, and it sounded perfect for Ronak. When I enrolled him, I was delighted to learn that the camp location was close to our home and happened to be a little beyond the Film City, a movie studio complex surrounded by wilderness in Mumbai. I had always known the Film City as an extension of the Aarey Colony area, but when I drove Ronak to camp, I was pleasantly surprised to see that kind of rich jungle in this quiet location. The landscapes had a refreshing and stimulating tropical feel, with green trees bedecked with the red and yellow frills of *gulmohar* flowers, which blossomed in summer. Driving past the Film City's gates, we reached the area reserved exclusively for BNHS. The center, surrounded by tall trees, featured a butterfly pavilion at the entrance. The staff welcomed all the parents and students as we arrived and introduced us to the camp's concept and activities. About a dozen excited adolescents assembled, beaming with enthusiasm and wonder.

All the campers with their parents were free to explore the trails around the center that day, and as we wandered, it struck me that this area was part of Sanjay Gandhi National Park (SGNP), the city's green zone, also known as the lungs of Mumbai. That meant it was home to many wild animals, including macaques, civets, barking deer, and hyenas, and I cringed, considering the dangers of such feral creatures. But the camp leaders assured us our children would be safe, emphasizing that forest guards patrolled the area round the clock, so we could relax as we bid our kids goodbye.

When we parents returned to the campsite to pick up our children on the final day, we were given an hour-long video presentation about the kids' activities. Suddenly, the projector flashed an image of a leopard, its eyes lit up with its own night-vision ability. The staff explained that the center filled the waterholes with water during the dry summer season so the animals might come by for a drink. One night, during a story-time session in the main room, one of the teachers had heard strange noises outside. She peered out the window, and, as she suspected, there was an adult leopard drinking out of the waterhole just fifteen feet away. She quietly beckoned all the campers to the window to witness that majestic sight unfolding right before their eyes. As soon as we heard, all the parents clapped in awe!

As the presentation continued, the staff informed us that SGNP had thirty-five leopards living on the premises, and that it was the only national park in India that lies within the city limits and therefore, was close to population centers.

"That's why we hear stories of leopards entering buildings, or sometimes being sighted in some slums," a parent chimed in.

"Sir, humans have encroached upon their habitat and shrunk the size of their homes," a volunteer patiently explained, "which forces them to wander into our neighborhoods."

Ronak was ecstatic. He had seen leopards several times in the zoo but had never seen a leopard in its natural habitat before. He still couldn't curb his enthusiasm, even after saying goodbye to his camp friends and teachers. "You know, Aai, they said that leopards rarely come this far to drink water by the center. We were all lucky," he marveled.

"Were you scared to see the animal just fifteen feet from the window?" I asked.

He shook his head. "No, I wasn't. We were inside, and if it charged, we could have closed the shutter. But I didn't think about that at the time. I was so focused, and the leopard just stared at us while drinking water."

"Yes, I could see its eyes reflecting the camera light," I concurred, thrilled that my son had had such a magical experience, and so close to home.

After that summer, SGNP became one of Ronak's favorite destinations in Mumbai. Over the years, he took countless hikes along the trails, enjoying the biodiversity of this jungle with his Nikon camera.

CR

30

Discrimination or Teasing?

Ding-dong, Ding-dong, Ding-dong. The doorbell rang three times. I sat sipping chai, enjoying my usual evening break on our balcony. Based on the three-ring pattern, it had to be Ronak at the door. He was a seventh grader now and had recently picked up this funny habit of ringing the bell three times. As I went to answer the door, I glanced at the clock and was surprised to find that the time was six-thirty p.m. This was strange—Ronak normally arrived home around seven-fifteen, so I had expected he would still be engrossed in playing soccer with his buddies from the apartment complex.

"Good evening, Ronak!" I greeted him at the door with a big smile.

"Hmm . . ." He nodded and walked directly to his room without looking at me.

I sensed something was troubling him. My "mom radar" pinged even harder when Ronak didn't even glance at the TV. On a typical day, he would come home after playtime and head straight for the TV. I usually had to remind him to wash his hands and feet and change clothes or take a bath before he hit the sofa with the TV remote in hand. His pat answer was always, "In five minutes," and I'd relent by bringing him strawberry milk while he surfed the myriad channels.

But today was so different. Looking downcast, Ronak simply walked to his room. I gave him a few minutes alone, then brought him strawberry milk. When I entered his room, I found him sitting in the chair on his balcony, peering down at his friends' soccer game. He seemed preoccupied, subdued.

Ronak took the glass and thanked me, but I could tell something was off. So, I pulled up a chair next to him and gently inquired, "So, how was the game?"

"Okay." He shrugged.

"How many goals did you score?"

"One, but then I was distracted by the teasing!" he blurted out.

My heart sank with his words and his worried expression. Cautiously, I urged him to tell me more.

"Mom, do you remember how you explained skin colors to me?"

I certainly did. How could I forget? Seven years ago, in Colorado back in 2005, Ronak had seemed sad and confused when he'd returned from a playdate with a kindergarten friend. "Why was Timothy bossing me around at his house?" Ronak had asked, looking hurt. "And he said something about my skin too."

I suspected racial discrimination, so I explained that God had created three different colors for human beings: cotton, wheat, and chocolate. "But God said, I'm very proud of all my creations, and you should be too. Love who you are, and don't let anyone tell you that you are small or insignificant based on your skin color." I emphasized that, in America, we often saw people of all races and skin tones coexisting, even if, sometimes, some people were treated differently just because of their complexions. "But you should never accept discrimination from anyone, nor should you be a party to it," I had instructed him, and then hoping to further ease my child's tender, troubled mind, I had added, "In India, the topic of skin color would not even matter."

At the time, I believed we would return to India someday, so I went one step further and told Ronak that discrimination based on race and color would never occur in India. And now, here we were in India, and my son was facing the issue head-on. Returning my focus to the present, I reminded myself, *Okay, but we are in India now.*

So, I asked Ronak, "Okay, what happened? Why did you remember that skin color incident?"

"Remember, you told me there would never be this kind of discrimination in India?" he said.

"Did someone say something to you, Ronak?" I probed, fearing what I might hear next.

"A new boy from our apartment building came to the soccer game," Ronak said. "Umesh is new and has a darker complexion. Today, when he missed a goal, some kids started teasing him based on his color. I was distracted and confused. You always taught me never to be a party to discrimination. I felt uncomfortable, and I left the game. I think some of those guys are racist."

"Oh! Okay . . ." I searched for the right words as I recalled other narratives that I had expressed to Ronak while we lived in Denver. Once, when Ronak was about five, Emily from his school, a beautiful little golden-haired girl around his age, came over for a playdate.

While they were playing a game of zoo animals, I overheard Emily suddenly blurt out, "Ronak, do you go to church?"

"No, we don't," he answered casually.

"Well, you should because if you don't, you will burn in hell!" she scolded, no doubt repeating what she'd heard elsewhere from the adults in her life. I quietly observed them from my kitchen table. Sounding even more curious, Emily asked, "Is it because you're not white?"

Speechless, Ronak had no ready response. Emily had explained what she'd been taught about how going to church was essential, and then they simply continued with their game. However, as soon as she left, Ronak immediately came to me with a series of questions. "Mom, why do we go to the temple?" he began.

Understanding the context of his conversation with Emily, I tried to comfort him with, "In India, people practice many religions, and the topic of faith doesn't even matter." I was still recalling that incident in Denver when Ronak's next question brought me back to the present.

"You never told me that they differentiate based on so many other things besides color here!" Ronak said. "Why do some people in my class tease the nonvegetarians?"

"They do?"

He nodded. "Yes, most of the class is vegetarian, and they scowl at nonvegetarians." Ronak seemed to possess a litany of examples proving my previous statements wrong. "I'm so surprised," he continued, sounding increasingly upset. "We are all brown people here, but they still discriminate based on skin color. Why? And they seem to categorize others based on language, food habits, and the areas and states people come from. Why?" Before I could formulate an appropriate answer, he exclaimed, "In my class, kids tease me and call me an 'English *babu*' because my Hindi is a little different."

I was floored. "That is so wrong," I said. "They shouldn't be doing this in school, or anywhere, for that matter. I am so sorry you had to hear that." I was hoping my words would comfort him a little.

Eager to ease his mind, I steered the conversation toward his homework to see if I could help him wrap it up quickly so he could get an early bedtime. After dinner, I allowed him a little extra TV time as a treat before kissing him goodnight.

Once he fell asleep, I took some time to sit quietly on the sofa and reflect on what he'd shared about the soccer game and being teased at school. *My son's been a victim of discrimination at school? Based on his language skills?* I pondered. *India is an independent country now, but are we really free of our language differences? Are we so different in terms of the food we eat or the clothes we wear? Here, we are always eager to categorize people based on their language, food, and state of origin.* But I stumbled upon another thought—it is human nature to classify people based on their differences; that's how we establish our identities as belonging to certain groups.

We want to talk about our differences, but conversely, we tend to seek out fellowship and companionship with people similar to ourselves. I remembered that when I had first moved to the U.S., I'd tried to make friends with people who shared my Indian origins.

I realized that when a person hailing from a different country experiences the same prejudice in other countries based on color, we call it racism. Still, when Ronak described the soccer game and how the other kids teased the new kid, Umesh, was Umesh a victim of discrimination? Maybe it was just a form of teasing. But Ronak, who had seen this kind of discrimination in the past, clearly saw signs of discrimination here. And he, himself, was being teased by classmates and treated differently based on his Hindi language skills. I felt so guilty. Why had I put my child in this situation? His distress left me questioning all the choices I had made three years ago in deciding to move.

At that time in America, there was a lot of awareness created about nondiscrimination right from the scholastic level. Ronak had mentioned that his fourth-grade class in Denver had students from different racial backgrounds, yet, even at the fourth-grade level, no one teased anyone by the color of their skin. Those days, American businesses and educational institutions were attempting to promote diversity and egalitarianism through legal and social pressure.

But in culturally diverse India, I realized that we, Indians, feel very proud of our ability to categorize people, beginning in child-hood. I suspect we find it easier to generalize about someone once we know what region or state that person comes from, along with what language he or she speaks, as India has many languages. As my grandma would say, "When we generalize those characteristics, it may help us uncover a common thread."

From my own personal experience, I've found that discrimination is not solely an Indian or American issue. Discrimination has no boundaries and does not stop at any national or regional border. Sadly, it exists in the mind of a person who chooses to practice it.

I recalled a conversation I'd had while on my morning walk about a month earlier. It was a hot and sunny morning when I reached the park at nine. I shortened my walk under intense sun-light and found some shade where I could stretch. Most of the usual walkers had finished their routes by now, but I noticed a new, curious face peering at me from the adjacent swing.

"Hi, I'm Sameera!" A woman in her late thirties with a ponytail approached and shook my hand. She was well dressed in exercise gear with color-coordinated leggings and top, and striking, orange shoes. I suspected she was from outside India.

"Nice to meet you. Where do you live?" I asked.

"In the brand-new building of the complex." Sameera glanced at my pedometer. "But we moved from Dubai," she added quickly.

"Welcome. We moved here from the United States," I said. "How do you like Mumbai?"

She pursed her lips, then continued cautiously. "People are not that friendly here, unlike us, Desis, living abroad."

I felt pleased to have found a kindred soul I could confide in. "Yes, I agree. We, Desis, living abroad are a different breed altogether. Not only are we friendly to our circle, but we're very helpful to other new Desis as well."

Sameera seemed to relax as she opened up further. "Coming to the homeland, you feel you will be well accepted, but that's when you realize that people discriminate against you as if you are an outsider in your birth country."

"Has someone treated you like that?" I frowned.

She nodded. "Yes. When you're new to the city, you tend to have many questions. But people here have no time for that. They seem annoyed by such 'mundane' questions, as if we should already know the answers since we're Indian."

I immediately recalled my own dreadful experience trying to hire a reliable maid. "I know what you mean. My own cousin had a judgmental response to my simple question about hiring and negotiating with a maid to help out at home."

For the next hour, I put my workout aside and helped this newcomer from Dubai, providing some what-to, how-to, and where-to advice with care and sympathy—just the way I had been helped by the Desis back when I had first arrived in the U.S.

છ

31

Society's Attitude Toward Men

The longer we lived in India, the more insight I gained into the new realities of contemporary Mumbai. One example in particular comes to mind.

Neeraj had just returned from a work trip to the U.S. in 2011. His flight landed around two-thirty a.m., and after clearing customs and immigration, he arrived home around four. After serving him a warm meal, I went to bed at about four-thirty a.m. I was still in my sweet, dreamy sleep when the maid rang the bell around eight a.m. Neeraj, still jet-lagged, was reading the newspaper in the living room, so he answered the door.

The maid was probably delighted to see Bhaiya ("brother"— what the maids called the male members of the households where they worked). Whenever Neeraj came home from a long trip, he always brought chocolates, and the maid knew that Didi would generously share the goodies with her. Neeraj told me later that as usual, she went into the kitchen to take care of the cookware and dishes first. Neeraj resumed his reading while I continued sleeping in on this relaxing Sunday morning. Ronak was fast asleep in his room, unaware that his dad was home.

The maid was still scrubbing dishes when Neeraj entered the kitchen a little later to prepare brunch for all of us, which was his Sunday ritual. The first step was making tea, so he took out the sugar and tea and heated the kettle. As the maid told me later, she quietly observed with a combination of admiration and awe to see a man willingly entering the kitchen and making tea! Neeraj told me that what she saw next nearly stopped her in her tracks—she even broke a glass! Quietly and confidently, Neeraj took the eggs out of the refrigerator, followed by bell peppers, mushrooms, and tomatoes because Ronak liked lots of vegetables in his omelet. As Neeraj rummaged for the knife and cutting board, the maid stopped washing dishes and joined in his search. She found the knife while Neeraj hunted down the board. My maid also confided that other men always asked for more help from the maid, like chopping the veggies or doing some extra cooking when their wives were not available to help in the kitchen.

As the maid resumed cleaning utensils, she couldn't quite grasp what she witnessed next. By now, Neeraj had finished dicing the vegetables into perfect cubes and whisked them together with some eggs in a bowl. He put the skillet on the stove and neatly added oil with no spills. The maid couldn't help but watch this cooking show by the man of the house. She probably hoped it would be entertaining, and she later told me that she'd almost prepared herself, thinking that she would have to guide Bhaiya on how to cook eggs.

As Neeraj proceeded to skillfully cook the omelets, she sneaked glances at his activities, expecting to see oil spilled and food burnt. When he poured whisked eggs evenly into the pan and, after the omelet fluffed up, effortlessly plated it without breaking it, she was astonished; Neeraj seemed to know all the tricks.

When Neeraj noticed her stare, he asked what was wrong. Embarrassed to have been caught gawking at his culinary skills, she quickly resumed her dishwashing.

By now, I had woken up to the sounds of the kitchen, and when I came out for breakfast, I was pleased to see the table filled with Neeraj's special omelets, cut fruits, and cereals, a beautiful reminder of our family's Sunday tradition. In my attempt to catch up on lost sleep, I had missed Neeraj's tour de force in the kitchen. I lovingly and happily gazed at Neeraj, wishing him good morning. Out of modesty, I refrained from a hug, concerned that the maid might faint upon seeing a husband and wife hugging in the kitchen. Although hugging is well accepted in the West, in the East, public displays of affection, even between married couples, are still frowned upon, especially in front of the help.

When Ronak saw his dad after two months, he began jumping for joy. "I'm so glad you're home, Baba!"

Neeraj happily hugged Ronak. Then, placing him on the chair, Neeraj quickly served his special breakfast.

"It's just like our weekend ritual, Mom," Ronak said happily. I smiled in agreement.

Eager to see what treats were hidden in Dad's bag, Ronak quickly devoured his breakfast in expectation of opening chocolates and other gifts.

I returned to the kitchen to serve the maid an omelet and tea. Seeing my cheerful mood, she got chatty and asked inquisitively, "Didi, how does Bhaiya know how to cook? He cooks so well."

Without thinking, I replied, "We've been cooking at home for several years." But then, noticing her clueless expression, I realized

I should have said "he" instead of "we," as, of course, the maid already assumed that I knew how to cook. So often, women's abilities are taken for granted and dismissed with a, "So what?" when compared with men's.

"You are lucky, Didi," the maid said, impressed with Neeraj's skills. Yet I sensed a shift in her tone and subtle facial expressions suggesting that it was wrong that the woman slept peacefully while the man of the house cooked. She was not alone in her thinking; most Indian households still considered it a crime for a man to cook. Even some of my acquaintances, on their evening walks, would stay late only if their husbands were busy at work; if the husbands were home, the wives were compelled to rush home to serve them dinner.

For myself, I was glad that Neeraj, even though he came from a conservative family, had picked up basic cooking skills in America. This transformation was a gift from America. Back in India, where few men deigned to even enter the kitchen, Neeraj practiced his cooking skills as time permitted.

In ways similar to this kitchen incident, I observed that men in this male-dominated society were granted more importance in all aspects of life. From the annual general meetings of the apartment building to the committee member meetings, even though this kind of discrimination does not exist on the books, in practice, they prefer female members to attend the meetings in the role of tacit approver, never raising their voices or asking questions. If you did raise a question, it might not be objected to, but the issue would be met with a cold shoulder and treated as a time-consuming distraction and would end up not being addressed. Yet, if any male member suggested something similar, it was immediately met with praise and attention.

Even when you visited a street vendor whose sole business depended on customers purchasing their goods, if you were a female, you would most likely be cast aside as soon as a male customer came along. Again, this may not have been intentional, but unconsciously, the hawker was conditioned to perceive any man as a potential paying customer and assume that a woman would automatically lack that power.

32

Going to the Movies

We'd been living in Mumbai for more than two years on that chilly Monday morning in November 2011. The sky was rosy with soft morning sunlight as I drove twelve-year-old Ronak to school for the Children's Day celebration.

Neeraj was back in the U.S. working on his latest project, so Ronak and I had lunch planned at Mom's after Ronak's half-day party at school. Mom suggested we take Ronak to the new 3-D movie in town, The Adventures of Tintin.[1]

So, in my quest to make it a fun and relaxing movie experience for Ronak, after dropping him off at school, I stopped by the multiplex to book advance tickets to the show. I figured a newly released kids' film might be packed on Children's Day.

"Do you need recliner seats?" the young woman behind the ticket window replied to my request to book four tickets for the evening show.

"How much does it cost for regular and recliner seats?" I asked.

"Only three hundred rupees [$6.90] for recliner."

I noticed she didn't quote the standard seating price. Having spent two years in Mumbai, I understood the dynamic and decided to push back a bit. "Could you show me the availability of seats on the screen?" I asked instead.

Gazing at the screen, I could see that the rest of the theater was empty except for the last two rows for that evening's show. It was clear we didn't need to pay extra for the special privilege of reclining seats, as Mom would have had to climb extra steps. So, I bought the tickets for regular seats in the front—at half the cost of the recliners. It felt good to know I was getting better and better at mastering the subtle intricacies of modern Mumbai life.

I was excited for the show that evening as I dressed in a comfortable, colorful *kurti* over jeans and even volunteered to drive to the movie theater. The theater was inside a mall that was only a ten-minute drive from Mom's, but in reality, it would take twenty to twenty-five minutes to get there, given peak evening rush-hour traffic.

Once we reached the mall, the fun began. Several vehicles waited at the entrance for parking ahead of us. Ronak was delighted to learn that his surprise was seeing a brand-new movie and he was even more excited that Grandma and my friend were coming along.

"I'm going to buy candies and popcorn or a hot dog at the movie!" he announced, perhaps imagining his complete movie experience.

"Hot dog? They don't sell hot dogs at the movies," my friend scoffed.

"No hot dog? Why not, Aai?" Ronak scowled. "I used to buy them in American theaters."

"Well, Ronak, at the theaters in India, we can get *samosas* and *batata vada*," I offered as consolation. "Do you remember how much

I missed those in America?" Thinking about my own former wistfulness for the foods of my homeland, suddenly I could relate to Ronak missing a typical American food item like a hot dog at the movies.

"Yes, I remember." Ronak nodded at the memory. "Do you know, Aaji, back in Colorado, Aai and Baba always mentioned *samosas* at least once at every movie."

"Yes," Mom confirmed, "*samosas* were your Aai's favorite food at the movies. She would pout if they ran out before we reached the sales counter."

In the meantime, the mall security guard motioned for us to roll down the windows. "Madam, unlock the bonnet and the dickey," the guard demanded.

"What?" Ronak snickered.

"He means the trunk of the car," I explained. "And the bonnet is the hood."

After taking a look under the hood and in the trunk, the guard handed over a parking stub to place in the parked car.

I drove toward the elevators, looking for a convenient parking spot, but the mall's security personnel posted every twenty feet were in charge and had decided that the parking structure needed to be filled from the farthest area first. So, they kept directing us forward and farther away from the elevators. The whole point of driving had been to park close enough to avoid a lengthy and uncomfortable walk for my mom. So, craning my neck out the window, I reasoned with the guard, asking for a spot near the elevator.

"Once this lot gets full, we are allowed to open the parking closer to the elevators. So, no," the guard decreed.

With no other choice, I drove into the only parking area open for us.

"Aai, it feels like going to Target and not being allowed to park near the entrance," Ronak said.

I agreed, feeling bewildered. "And that, too, was because their parking staff decided to fill the farthest parking spots first."

By the time I parked the car, I was a little annoyed, but my mom and friend seemed unaffected by it.

"The security guard is posted to guide you. Why are you questioning their help?" my friend chimed in as we passed through security scanners to enter the mall from the basement parking.

Once inside the mall, we searched for the elevators but only found one that was assigned to mall staff; so, our only option was the escalator. Unfortunately, we soon realized we had to exit on each floor and find the escalator at the other end of the mall, which involved significant walking for my elderly mom.

"Let's look for elevators so Mom can be comfortable. That way, she doesn't have to run with us, and we'll get there on time." The movie was starting soon, so I felt some urgency.

"What's the big deal?" my friend countered.

"We can take the escalators," my mom also agreed.

"But then we'll miss the beginning of the movie." Ronak looked worried.

So, we asked about elevators, but the only one was located at the far corner of that floor. My main concern was Mom walking that distance, so I held her hand and slowed my pace to walk beside her as we headed there. When we finally reached the third floor, we again had to go through security before entering the theater. There were separate entries for men and women, and our female security personnel instructed us to open our bags. As I complied, she stirred the items in my purse with her bare hands.

"Phew," I muttered.

"They already screened us at the ground floor security desk," my friend complained. She'd been unaffected so far, but this second security check raised her ire.

I reminded her, "Don't worry. They're just doing their jobs."

At the theater entrance, a uniformed employee stood holding a bucket of 3-D glasses and asked, "Ma'am, do you want refundable glasses or permanent glasses?"

We asked for the refundable glasses, and he handed us four unwrapped pairs, which surprised me. "So, are these disinfected?" I asked.

"Yes." He nodded quickly, looking anxious to move on to the next customer.

Hmm. I considered the dozens of glasses piled in his basket along with the number of people crowding into the theater and doubted there'd been time to clean and disinfect the glasses from the previous show. Nevertheless, we reluctantly paid and grabbed our glasses. Fortunately, I had a small bottle of sanitizer in my purse, which we used to clean them.

The decor in these new multiplex theaters was impressive compared to what I remembered from my childhood, and even Ronak remarked, "These are Maharaja-style seats," as he touched the extra-soft velvet on our chairs' bright red seat covers.

Before the movie began, we made a quick trip to the concession stand, where both Ronak and I were disappointed to find that the popcorn was already "butter-flavored," but there was no option for the customer to add more butter. Since we loved to bathe our popcorn in butter, this surprised me, as these new Mumbai multiplex theaters were modeled after American movie theaters but still lacked melted-butter dispensers. But perhaps it didn't matter when there were so many delicious Indian and other food options to choose from instead—*samosas, vada,* corn *chaat,* sandwiches, pizza, ice cream, and beverages.

"Ma'am, I'm out of change," the person behind the concession window said. "The movie is starting, so share your screen and seat number, and I will bring the change."

Balancing the popcorn, *samosas,* and tea on one tray, I impatiently agreed.

I hoped that he would bring my change during the intermission, but instead, he interrupted us in the middle of the movie. Soon, as if drawn to a magnet, more serving staff kept coming to other seats, delivering food orders, walking to the middle of a row to reach a particular seat number, then standing tall and blocking others' view. Nevertheless, the customers who ordered food and those who had to adjust their seats for the serving staff seemed unconcerned, as did my mom and friend. I admired their patience.

Although Ronak and I did not enjoy the interruptions and commotion, we were compensated generously by the unfolding of that popular comic book story on the screen. As the movie ended, even before the credits began to roll, everyone stood up, and some even left their seats, crowding the aisle in their rush to depart. This, at least, was something I did recall from my childhood.

"Why the hurry?" Ronak frowned, and my mom, my friend, and I immediately agreed.

It took Ronak, Neeraj, and me some time to adjust to these social and cultural differences and truly feel at home in Mumbai.

◌ৎ

33

Coveted Tiger Safari

"When will the tiger come?" a middle-aged man sitting in the safari jeep alongside ours broke the silence in the middle of the jungle. It was during our family excursion to Tadoba Tiger Reserve in the summer of 2012. The man was growing impatient with the excruciating wait, as were Neeraj, Ronak, and I.

The guide in that vehicle hushed the grumbler with his hand and whispered, "Alarm call."

He pointed at the treetops a little north of us and directed our attention to the noisy monkeys moving in the branches.

"The sambar is calling," our guide continued in a whisper. We could hear a distant sambar deer grunt from the left side of the dense green patch ahead.

That was the second sambar call, and I thought, *I should at least be able to see the sambar deer by now. I've come all this way to see them, not just hear their calls.*

At that moment, a peacock wailed in the distance.

"The tiger was set to come here, but he suddenly went into the left side of the jungle," our guide explained.

How do you know that? I wondered.

The guide answered as though he'd heard my thoughts. "When we heard the first sambar deer call, it warned others that it had seen the tiger in our proximity and to be alert." The guide added, "That's why we waited so long in that location. But when the monkeys ahead of us continued the calls, they confirmed seeing the tiger proceed. Sometime later, we also heard the second sambar deer in the left woods, which indicated the tiger turning left. The wailing peacock also confirmed that the predator was moving ahead, away from us."

Wow! That animal language seemed fascinating as they painted a virtual map of the tiger's location for each other. At the same time, they watched out for all the other animals surrounding them.

As we grasped this information, we all noticed a gaur, a type of Indian bison, in the deep woods. It stood attentive and wide-eyed, looking enormous and stout in its dark brown-burgundy color.

The guide signaled our driver to move the jeep slowly toward the left patch, the site where we heard the sambar and the peacock. As we drove through that typical central Indian forest, the striking red *mahua* flowers stood out against the green foliage, vying for our attention.

A little ahead, where the road bent, we finally saw the sambar standing alert behind a tree. Two jeeps were already waiting when we reached the spot. The growing number of jeeps in the area made it evident that the guides' network was active. We were likely to see the arrival of Yeda Anna any minute, the oldest tiger living in Tadoba National Park in the state of Maharashtra.

Soon, as we heard other bird calls, smiles flashed across the faces in the jeeps. With bated breath, we all looked intently in the direction where we'd seen the sambar. Suddenly, our guide, standing above his seat and looking through his binoculars, pointed toward the south. As we looked back, peering through those seven jeeps parked on each side of the dirt road . . . there he was! The tiger walked slowly and majestically toward the north. Striding past all the jeeps behind us in his elegant style, he ignored all the vehicles and the people in them, yet demanded everybody's rapt attention. When the tiger walks, everything in the jungle seems to come to a standstill. Each of us was dumbfounded, basking in all his royalty and grandeur and in return, offering our great reverence for the king of the jungle.

The sight of him gave me goosebumps as he walked past our jeep, slowly yet sturdily. I felt terrified and vulnerable, sitting exposed in an open jeep and close to this enormous wild cat. The guide assured us that we were safe as long as we stayed in the jeep because the tiger viewed all of us and the vehicle as a single entity. Thus, the tiger never considered us as part of its food chain, and we breathed a sigh of relief.

No matter how aggressive and carnivorous such a creature could be, we were still awestruck by the presence of this big Bengal tiger. His fur looked like a royal shawl with mustard, yellow, orange, and black stripes. As he stepped through the sunbeams, the fur brightened like an exotic design. It was so regal!

Considering his tongue rolling over his mouth through his lethally sharp teeth, it appeared he was probably finding a resting spot after a heavy meal. He continued past us and then lay down under the bamboo trees. Finally, everyone was ecstatic to have seen the tiger; even the no-tiger-yet man in the next vehicle had a gratified smile.

Our guide later told us that the tiger's name, Yedda Anna, meant a mad older brother. He said they'd added "mad" because this tiger was known to randomly charge at jeeps in the past. With age, he had calmed down a bit. Luckily, by the time we heard this, we had exited Yedda Anna's territory, so we could all digest this information without getting troubled by it.

As we continued our safari ride to the next attraction, I remembered that after our move, Neeraj, Ronak, and I had witnessed India's biodiversity and forest wealth during our jungle vacations to Bandipur and Ranthambore National Parks. Considering Ronak's initial sadness postmove and his interest in wildlife, I was on a quest to get Ronak interested and engaged more and more in our current country of residence. As time passed, our interest in the subject evolved into a love for Indian wildlife, and we craved seeing the main attraction in Indian jungles: the Bengal tiger. Hoping to see this majestic big cat in its natural habitat, we researched India's top national parks that offered tiger safaris. Since tiger tourism is popular, the safaris sell out quickly. Private cars are forbidden to enter the national parks, and only park-authorized jeeps have permits to drive through the jungle. So, we quickly learned the importance of planning a tiger safari vacation well in advance.

We were now nearing Tadoba Lake, surrounded by green vegetation. We could see a herd of deer happily grazing on the grass and a few egrets standing tall on the edge of the lake, while the scaly backs of crocodiles floated across the water. This area was a paradise for bird watchers. A flock of wading birds roosted on the tree beside the lake; a black drongo swiftly splashed over the water as though catching something. As we turned our attention from branch to branch, the guide pointed out green barbets, coppersmith barbets, Indian white-eyes, and a yellow-fronted woodpecker. The birds' vibrant colors left us speechless. The guide pointed out an Indian roller making a short flight with the morning sunrays highlighting all the colors on its wings. This corner patch near the lake was a mesmerizing site full of these diversely colored birds. The main objective of the early morning safari, we were told, was to take in the first movements of morning awakening in the jungle. The birds are intensely active with the rising sun. I had never been a morning person, and yet that day, I'd been thrilled to wake up to the alarm while it was still dark and make it to the open jeep for the early morning safari.

"Hear that *tonk, tonk, tonk* sound? It's a coppersmith barbet working on the tree," our guide whispered. A *bhardwaj* majestically flew in the distance; he looked magnificent.

Soon, we halted at a safe spot for a quick breakfast and unwrapped our sandwiches and juice boxes packed by the hotel. Meanwhile, our driver and guide continued networking with other safari jeeps, who shared their day's tiger-spotting experiences along with the locations. Based on that information, this duo strategized which tiger was more likely to be visible, and soon, our jeep headed in that direction. Our guide mentioned they would take us on a longer ride for a rare sighting of a male tiger living with its cubs.

"But male tigers always stay away from the cubs, don't they?" Ronak asked immediately.

Seeing Ronak's knowledge of the subject, the guide happily supplied more information. "The male tiger named Waghdoh is back to care for his four cubs, and I am told they are currently resting in that place. And if we are lucky, we can see this miracle of nature."

After the morning excitement of seeing our very first tiger in that jungle, we were now more observant of the park's flora as the jeep sped down the road. The rain-fed streamlets ran along the tar road, which resembled a giant snake. We noticed the change in the vegetation as we proceeded to Waghdoh's area of the tiger reserve. The forest featured tall, deciduous trees, such as teaks, *mahua*, and bamboo. As soon as we reached the location amid the bamboo vegetation, we spied that big alpha male resting in the shade. He sat imperially and calmly like a true king of the jungle. Before our jeep came to a complete halt, we caught a glimpse of the four adorable cubs lying and playing in the dirt, sheltered behind the father. It was a rare sighting indeed, but when we wondered aloud about the tigress' whereabouts, our guide was clueless. We noticed two other jeeps waiting nearby, their occupants clicking pictures, and a few more arriving, proving that the news had spread quickly on the guides' safari network. This time, we were not scared to be so close to the tiger, even though he was in his prime and much heavier than the older tiger we had seen earlier that day.

After watching the cute little cubs drop to the ground, tired from their active playtime, we decided to turn back. The guide heard reports of a new area where another tiger had recently been spotted. As we turned to head back, a black bear crossed our path within a few seconds. We stopped and quietly observed the sloth bear ambling across the road with a slow swing of its rear end. Now prepared with his 500mm camera lens, Ronak started snapping photos, hoping to capture the amazing images.

Nothing before our eyes was staged or choreographed; we were about to witness the unfolding of a natural, spontaneous jungle law—ruling his kingdom, the tiger maintains the rhythm of the jungle while sitting on top of the food chain.

Soon, the bear changed its mind and returned to the same side of the road where the Waghdoh tiger family sat. It slowly walked toward the pond that was a few meters away from the Waghdoh family. Just then, one of the tired cubs lazing around the father picked himself up and curiously went after the bear, soon followed by the three other cubs. Later, we could hear distressed cries from the bear; probably it was being chased. After hearing those calls, the tiger dad quickly joined the cubs, and we witnessed a live jungle kill in progress. Suddenly, the tigress, who was hidden from the onlookers, emerged from the bushes to join her family in the hunt. It felt as if we were watching a *National Geographic* documentary. Loud and graphic, it nonchalantly unfolded partially in front of our eyes and partially behind the tall vegetation. We were speechless and focused intently on the scene. Ronak was so excited that he forgot all about his camera and instead, captured the scene in his memory.

We thoroughly enjoyed this mesmerizing experience and were delighted to learn about these new parts of India, as we had never visited these jungle interiors before. Being exposed to the wildlife, we felt vulnerable, yet loved the incredible adventure.

Yeda Anna, an old male tiger in Tadoba National Park, 2012.

ॐ

34

New Acquaintances and
Lasting Friendships

Slowly, as I navigated through the many challenges of our new life in Mumbai, I began to feel ready to socialize and explore new friendships.

These friends helped me find my footing as I adjusted to living in a changed Mumbai. I made friends with other moms grappling over family and child-rearing responsibilities, and they, in turn, comforted me while offering a fresh perspective on my child's progress or obstacles.

At the same time, there were those who helped reinvigorate my love for my birthplace. One evening, on my daily walk in the podium park, I encountered a very reserved yet needy-looking face. She flashed a brief smile and introduced herself. As we strolled around the garden, we engaged in typical chitchat like, "Where are you from?" and, "Which building do you live in?" As she grew more comfortable in our conversation, she opened up rather boldly, expressing her frustrations about living in crowded, fast-paced Mumbai.

"What kind of city is this? And the schools? Oh, my God!" she said abruptly.

"Why? What's wrong with the schools?" I asked, alarmed and hoping for more insight.

She rolled her eyes. Comparing apples to oranges, she said, "The schools are not good in Mumbai. There are no schools like Delhi's." Emboldened now, she continued, "And people talk funny here."

It was true that Mumbai residents spoke relatively quickly compared to Americans, as Marathi's tempo and flow differ from English—but this woman from India's capital city found the locals' speech not just fast but weird as well. I was curious. "Talk funny? How so?" Soon, I realized my mistake in uttering my thoughts out loud.

She sighed dramatically. "The funny language? People say *Tu* instead of *Aap*. They have no manners."

Aha! Now I recognized her arrogance; she viewed Mumbai as beneath her.

This caught my attention as she talked about my birth city and mother tongue. I couldn't just let her remarks slide; I took it upon myself to explain why she was wrong.

"My dear, the Marathi *Bombaiya* language does not have words like *Aap* for people who are the same age. *Aap* is reserved for an elderly person, so you, being younger, don't hear that word addressed to you," I explained, delighted to defend both Mumbai and my mother tongue.

Although this woman came from Delhi, a major metropolitan city, she utterly lacked knowledge of Marathi, yet she made no attempt to understand the language before judging and condemning it. I had stood on the other side of that fence when I was new to the United States. Despite knowing standard British English all my life, I made it incumbent upon myself to learn American English—words like "apartment" for "flat," "elevator" for "lift," "okra" for "ladies' fingers," "mailman" for "postman," and "faucet" for "tap," just to name a few differences.

In contrast to this acquaintance from Delhi, some of my new friends in Mumbai were amusing. There was one funny incident when seven of us women were planning a surprise birthday party for our friend, Shanti. After we finished the planning, Manisha, worried about her upcoming European trip, asked my advice on how to dress and what to pack for London. I had just returned from my own European vacation and was happy to assist.

"Well, London gets very cloudy, gloomy, and cool, so layers are great for the weather's mood swings."

But Falak, who was usually quiet, suddenly lit up. "No, you don't have to worry, Manisha," she reassured her. "There's cream available there, and when you put it on, you don't feel cold at all."

"What?" we all asked quizzically.

Falak nodded enthusiastically. "Oh, yes. When our Bollywood actresses go to Switzerland to shoot song-and-dance scenes in the snowy mountains, they slather this cream around their halter tops before dancing in chiffon *sarees*, and it keeps them warm."

How to respond to that?

"Have you used it in Switzerland?" Anita asked, almost in a reflex.

"No, we haven't been there, but I heard it somewhere," Falak answered confidently.

Incredulous, we all stared at her. I mentioned that I believed those were the occupational hazards those actresses had learned to accept. I also added that if it were true, it would have been nicer if I could have just put on that lotion rather than layers and layers of clothing to endure the Colorado cold.

The best friendships lasted a lifetime. These friends appeared from all walks of life. Some wanted to learn my techniques for keeping fit, although I never considered myself fit. Others offered support when I was alone with Ronak, especially when he suffered a hand fracture for the second time while Neeraj worked abroad.

Some friends hosted a surprise birthday party for me at a club! I remember dancing the night away with my girlfriends to tuneful English and Hindi music.

I really appreciated the friends who taught me how to enjoy a party—that when you host a party in a living room packed with furniture and many guests, you can manage to steal a few moments to dance with your spouse. However, I cringed the first time I attended a party in one friend's apartment, where all four walls were decorated with souvenirs. A crowd of at least seventeen people huddled in her living room with drinks in our hands and swarmed the appetizers set out in two places. It made me think about our Colorado parties in our spacious houses, yet we always sent the kids to the basement for their playtime and kept the entire living space open for the party. But I must admit that parties were always fun with our friends, whether in Denver or Mumbai.

My new friendships permeated all aspects of my life. Some friends confided their tips for managing the help and even shared their recipe secrets. Some offered me company at the Holi Festival during the rain dance under the sprinklers hung above the venue. At the same time, some clapped, whistled, and shouted "Once more!" to the songs I sang onstage. At times, we got together to watch the famous *Dandiya* celebrations or a good Hindi play at Prithvi Theatre.

One special friend visited us on Christmas Day with sweets upon learning that we decorated a Christmas tree every year and celebrated the holiday even after moving to India. Some admired the *rangolis* I made during Diwali and encouraged me. And then, some new to Mumbai, traveled with me to South Mumbai for the Kala Ghoda Art Festival celebrations.

Insightful friends helpfully shared their business management tips, and we wholeheartedly supported each other in assessing each other's goals during our Sunday meetings while brainstorming investment ideas and time management strategies.

All in all, a few friends later drifted away into their busy lives, while others stayed friends for life. I still cherish all those friendships and even receive phone calls on my birthday from a few. These relationships taught me that we, humans, are all the same; we want to be respected and heard, and to express ourselves. Those who remain friends forever, I realized, are there to absorb the shocks, smooth the rough edges, or lend a listening ear and a sympathetic shoulder. They're the people who steer you back onto the path of happiness when some "well-wishers" push you off track.

CR

35

High School Years in Juhu

In 2015, Ronak was accepted into a new International Baccalaureate (IB) high school. I had learned that schools in that part of town, Juhu, had more immigrants from other countries with similar socioeconomic backgrounds, so Neeraj and I felt comfortable enrolling him there. However, since the new school year began, Ronak had been spending more time commuting and more time doing homework with little downtime. The IB curriculum was grueling, but from what Ronak said, he seemed to be adjusting to it all right. Soon enough, it was time for the midsemester parent-teacher conference. I was anxious about attending since this would be my first time meeting Ronak's high school teachers and the other parents.

My first task was to call Sitaram, our driver from a driver-for-hire company. Depending on the commute, I would hire this driving service for a day. Although driving was not an issue for me at this point, finding a parking spot near the school around dismissal time was a big challenge and quite a drill.

Next, I had to decide what to wear, ideally something comfortable while also giving a presentable motherly vibe to make a good first impression on Ronak's teachers. In glamorous Mumbai, women wore contemporary Western or Indian outfits, but going to Juhu in particular, I narrowed it down to a Western dress. Somehow, I felt compelled to dress like the majority of Juhu residents, who leaned toward modern and stylish clothes. My motivation was clear: I wanted to fit in.

"Good morning, ma'am!" Sitaram greeted me. "Where are we going today?"

This simple question reignited my anxiety. "Going to Juhu." I was perplexed by my own thinking and felt concerned about the commute ahead. I knew the drive would be long, so I brought some audiobooks and music CDs. While the music played, I jotted down a few questions for Ronak's teachers. I was especially curious about his adjustment to his new school and new friends.

Occasionally, I glanced out the window to gauge how far we'd come. The busy streets, vehicles, traffic lights, and tall, clustered buildings all seemed like pieces of a puzzle, and I was glad I wasn't driving. The traffic soared with the rising temperature and sky-rocketing humidity. Back when I was about Ronak's age, I also commuted to Juhu, to attend Mithibai College. Now, though, the journey seemed long and exhausting.

At last, after about fifty minutes dodging throngs of autorick-shaws, scooters, and assorted four-wheelers through the urban sprawl, we reached Ronak's school. As Sitaram pulled the car up to the main gate, the security guards signaled for him to make it a quick drop-off. I was thankful my driver was in charge of safely getting the car out of there. Cautiously, I stepped out of the vehicle.

In the top-floor auditorium, I saw a few moms already present. I immediately realized I'd been wrong about the dress code; not everyone wore Western outfits, and two moms were dressed in Punjabi suits. The teacher's absence posed an excellent opportunity for me to communicate with other class parents, mostly moms.

I shared a big, square, eight-seater table with five other moms; three sat huddled closely on my left side in a triangle shape, chatting with each other. The rest of us sat on the remaining sides of the table and introduced ourselves. One mom asked me my child's name, and I casually answered, "Ronak," assuming they were just trying to make conversation.

But, to my astonished delight, another mom jumped in. "I hear he's really good at English and makes lovely sketches!"

Reflexively, I asked her child's name.

"Kanchan!" she answered, adding, "My daughter also tells me that Ronak likes to play soccer too."

I was amazed, not only that her daughter had shared so much information in so little time—school had started only two months ago—but also that this fellow mom cared enough to remember Ronak's name and characteristics. I felt instant admiration for her. But my joy was tempered by the awkward realization that Ronak never shared anything about his class, let alone his classmates' unique qualities. And even if he had shared any details, I would not have been able to associate the characteristics with his classmates' names.

So, I replied, "Thank you, that's so sweet of your daughter." I smiled softly, hoping to hide any awkwardness that might have been visible on my face.

As we conversed, I learned that the three moms clustered together lived near the school, and their kids had attended the same school since kindergarten.

That explains why they're so friendly with each other, I thought, *enough to discuss something in hushed voices, completely cold-shouldering others at the table.*

Meanwhile, the conversation among the rest of us turned to the teachers and what our kids thought about them. Suddenly, one of the moms sitting in the chairs clustered together turned her attention toward me. Dressed in her blue *salwar kurta* with her long hair and dangling silver earrings, she tossed her hair and, looking at me sideways, asked, "Where do you live? Are you closer to school?"

"We don't live close to the school," I answered nonchalantly. "We live in the Western suburb of Malad. But, for the IB curriculum, we don't mind the commute."

The facial expressions of the mom trio seemed to change quickly, ranging from disbelief to disdain.

"If you don't live in Juhu, then how did your son get admitted to our school?" the woman in the blue dress asked imperiously. It felt as if nothing mattered to her except where we resided.

I was disappointed by her attitude; here I was, minding my own business yet trying my best to fit in as a parent in this new school. When we had left the U.S. for India without batting an eye, we'd just been happy to be in Mumbai, but she seemed to be judging us because we didn't live in Juhu. I was incredulous. In my mind, I ran through several scenarios of how I might answer this pseudo-intellectual mom.

I might have said, "Well, he got admitted here with the same enthusiasm with which we came to India from the topmost economy of the world."

But I chose to stick to a less dramatic and highly factual answer more pertinent to that audience. "My son came to this school based on his merits." I answered calmly and confidently. "He passed the entrance exam and was proudly welcomed by three panel members after acing the interview."

In reality, that parent probably had no clue. Since their children came from the same school, those privileged kids did not have to undergo entrance exams and interviews like other students did for the IB curriculum. Proving my theory, the blue-suited mom shrugged and offered nonchalantly, "Oh, I thought admission was based on where you live."

My Dad always reminded me of a good piece of advice often attributed to Mark Twain— "Never argue with fools; onlookers may not be able to tell the difference."[1]—keeping that in mind, I chose not to stoop to her level and instead, just got up from the table and gracefully walked away to mingle with other new parents who had come in during this conversation.

Soon, the kids arrived in the auditorium after the end of the school day, and a tap on my shoulder made me turn around. It was Ronak. "Aai, look!" He sounded excited as he handed me his report card.

I felt a little anxious as I opened the card. This new IB curriculum of international stature was challenging; in addition, I worried that the school schedule and long commute left Ronak barely any time to study. I needn't have worried. As I read the report card, I smiled to see that Ronak's grades were excellent in this new curriculum, with no apparent adverse reflection of his study time crunch.

When we first moved to India, I thought about the competitive nature of parents there and realized that considering the country's huge population, the number of better opportunities for advancement was limited, so naturally, parents honed in on academics;

that's why Indian kids get sent to subject tutors and extra coaching classes at an early age. I understood that kids were much smarter on this side of the globe because of those factors, and I worried about Ronak.

But after our move, Neeraj and I agreed that no matter the circumstances, we would not succumb to the pressure of private tuition enrollments and would never demand that Ronak prove himself to be the best student in class. As parents, we always refrained from demanding 100 percent on his report card. Instead, we encouraged him for his 100 percent efforts and were happy even if he got 80 percent rather than 95.

With these thoughts in mind, I slowly moved along with Ronak toward the classrooms to meet his teachers. Fortunately, all the teachers I met that day graciously allayed my worries and praised Ronak for being a well-behaved and attentive student. I was proud of my gallant warrior, well-adjusted now, even in his second school in India. His success was all due to his intense efforts, especially his focus, careful observation, and politeness. His teacher said that those same qualities paired with adaptability made him a good student in the classroom. By now, he liked being in India, although he had never complained about the transition.

On our way home, relaxing in our air-conditioned car, I contemplated the stark contrast in my experiences that day: the reassuring way the teachers had warmed up to Ronak, and the Juhu mom's narrow-minded thinking. It seemed strange that both had happened in the same school.

On hearing about my experience earlier in the day, Ronak nodded in understanding. "When one of the Juhu-based students asked me where I lived and I answered, 'Malad,' he asked, 'Where is that?' Some of my classmates don't know where Malad is, even though they've lived in Mumbai since childhood."

This sounded sadly familiar. Yet I thought the blue-dressed mom had exhibited absurd pride, behaving like a self-appointed gate-keeper to bar any outsider. But by now, I understood that I had to expand my point of view and just ignore such petty comments so I could continue my successful adjustment to the present Mumbai.

Besides, I was more focused on Ronak's progress in IB, and Neeraj and I were quite impressed with it. In this school as a fine arts student, Ronak successfully showcased a themed exhibition of eleven large canvases, one of which was a three-dimensional work of art. His teachers and the audience were in awe, and we couldn't have been prouder. The best part was that my mom also visited this art exhibition to pat him on the back.

After earning his IB diploma, Ronak opted for a gap year before starting his undergraduate degree. He spent much of that year traveling around different parts of India. He volunteered for several weeks at a research center in Agumbe, where he got to see a lot of reptiles and amphibians he'd never encountered before and ended up getting bitten by a Malabar pit viper. In the hot, dry forests of Northern Telangana, he participated in the all-India tiger census.

In the fall, he spent a month backpacking in the Northeastern states of Assam and Arunachal, where he came across rhinos, tigers, gibbons, and more than three hundred species of birds. He then had an opportunity to go down to the Anamalai Mountains in Tamil Nadu to work for a biologist and spent the month conducting amphibian surveys along mountain streams winding through tea estates, coffee estates, and shola forests.

CR

PART FOUR

The Treasure I Found in India

36

The Enticing Side of India

"You are already enough!" our instructor uttered clearly and distinctly before the meditation class. He explained that they conducted those sessions not because the students lacked something but because the organizers aspired to improve the quality of life of each one of us with that training.

His words were music to my ears. By 2013, I found myself facing a challenging time. I was in a sad emotional state for a year while my mom was recovering after two surgeries. I was glad I could be close by during her illness and take care of her rather than being so far away in Denver and helplessly worrying about her. I had hoped she would come to stay at my apartment to recover after her surgeries, and I had even decided to hire full-time household help so I could care for Mom while still tending to my other responsibilities. But Mom entirely rejected my offer. She felt she'd recover better in her own home, where she was most comfortable. So, it remained a stressful time, especially as Neeraj was on a work assignment in the U.S., while I was taking care of our household, my work, Ronak's routine, his school test preparations, and then going to Mom's place to look after her and give my siblings a break. It was tough functioning on all fronts. What felt most punishing was that in spite of living near Mom's area, I did not have the opportunity to care for her full-time during her recovery as I had hoped.

So, when I heard the instructor's reassuring words during this meditation session, it felt like a weight off my shoulders. For many months while my mom was ill, I had felt like I could not handle everyone around me. I was already scared of losing Mom during her illness, so every demand my relatives placed on me added to the burden, making me feel like I could not measure up to their expectations. Those four magical words—"You are already enough!"— brought me home and set me free. They made me aware of how I walked a thin line between self-torture and losing myself in pleasing others, trying to meet all kinds of rational and irrational demands. Suddenly, I grew very emotional at the recitation of those magical words.

After three to four years in India, I realized that the pace of the city and the sheer volume of people tend to push you constantly to keep up with the city's rhythm. Eventually, you fall prey to the rat race mentality and the idea of having to chase time. Consequently, you end up feeling exhausted.

"Why don't you come this Sunday to the auditorium?" one of our friends suggested in the fifth year of our stay in India. "You can certainly benefit and take away something meaningful with you." But Neeraj and I hesitated initially, thinking it might be one of those multilevel-marketing product meetings. Nevertheless, we couldn't refuse a friend, so we reluctantly joined the forum.

The event turned out to be an introductory session to a course on *pranayama* and meditation. I was intrigued by the methods discussed in that first session, and before it ended, I decided to dive into this experience for the next fourteen days. The only downside was that I would have to reach the venue at six-thirty a.m. sharp for the next two weeks. I was very hesitant about the time; however, once the training began, I witnessed the benefits within three days. I felt lighter and more energetic, breathed fully, and finally was able to get up early without a sweat.

During those sessions, the instructor guided us through practicing *pranayama* and meditation techniques, along with some fascinating question-and-answer sessions that dug deep into the human psyche. While they served breakfast that was made fresh and entirely of what they called "*Sattvic* food" (fresh vegetarian food), they also encouraged us to continue a vegetarian diet at home for two weeks. And the effects were immensely positive; feeling energized, I experienced fewer aches.

After those two weeks, as part of the program and to deepen our understanding, we had a three-day, Friday-to-Sunday retreat to a very self-sustained ashram in the hills outside Pune. The instructors explained that fully immersing our bodies and minds in that blissful experience was imperative. However, soaking in this new spiritual, magical energy meant leaving Neeraj and Ronak at home. As we assembled that Friday morning, most of us professionals—professors, surgeons, IT professionals, businessmen, and restaurateurs—had to manage one day away from work. I was excited but a little skeptical, as I was going away with just a few acquaintances I had made during those fourteen days.

The Mumbai-Pune expressway glided through the scenic Sahyadri mountain range. Slowly, everyone began to open up to the group as our two-hour bus trip unfolded. Once off the highway in Pune, we continued our journey toward this unknown village that surrounded the ashram. Eagerly awaiting our destination, we watched the foliage, fields, and hills on the way. Little did we know that once we arrived at our destination, our cell phones would be confiscated after one final call to our families to provide them with the ashram's number in case of an emergency. Once seized, our phones became the ashram's property for the next three days.

The ashram was a pleasing sight, perched on top of the hill amid trees and various bushes. The facility used grains and other resources from the villages located at the foot of the mountain and also grew different fruit trees and vegetable patches in the surrounding area. While touring the premises, we realized that there were no TVs or radios, at least in the shared access areas.

The ashram lifestyle was certainly a change of pace for us modernized, digitized, fast-paced city dwellers. Here, we all slept in the open hall with a terra-cotta roof overhead and stashed our belongings in cubbies in a small space adjacent to the hall to forget about them until we actually needed something. The staff prepared us to connect well with ourselves, disconnect from outside stimuli, cultivate self-reliance, and become part of the bigger purpose while there, putting aside our "me, my, mine" thinking. We would participate in group activities designed by the ashram curriculum to strengthen these principles.

The bedding provisions had been kept on the floor for women on one side of the hall and men on the opposite side. So, the first task in self-reliance was to prepare our beds. The ashram had recommended bringing warm blankets from home because nights on the mountain would get colder. I was grateful that I'd brought our zero-degree sleeping bag, as, during the night, I witnessed a few unprepared individuals shivering, covered only by their thinner shawls. Our experience camping in Colorado's colder fall season really came in handy.

After the long bus ride and eventful day, we went to bed close to midnight. But no matter how lightly or deeply one slept after that exhausting day, the following morning, at five-fifteen a.m., instrumental sitar music began to play at a low volume for the first five minutes, then gradually rising to a big crescendo, making sure everyone was up. The lights were switched on to compensate for the dark, wintry sky.

"Roll the bedding and put it away to keep the area open. You have thirty minutes to complete your morning rituals and return to the group," a man in his early twenties instructed in his commanding voice. He had seemed very quiet on our bus journey the day before, but this morning, we learned that he was an accomplished associate instructor.

On that cold January morning, I returned dressed in my yoga gear, freshened up after brushing my teeth with ice-cold water. I found the hall ready for the morning session. A tape of a light *Om* recitation hummed in the background. Jute carpets covered the entire floor, and our main *guruji* sat in *vajrasana* (sitting on folded legs), facing east. The associate instructor summoned everyone to join in rows aligned behind *guruji* in the same *asana* on the floor. I was happy to comply, recalling that just two weeks earlier, I had been reluctant even to sit cross-legged on the floor due to my knee condition, but the intervening fourteen days had worked like an elixir. Now, sitting on the floor in a difficult *vajrasana,* with a little help from a pillow under my folded legs, I was able to join the whole congregation.

We began our first session by practicing the *pranayama* we had learned over the previous fourteen days, except now, we were ensconced in nature, breathing in the cold, crisp, early morning air, facing east as if to welcome the sun. It was a spectacular sight watching the sunrise, its magical touch turning all the trees and greenery to gold while we simultaneously practiced this ancient Indian technique, perfecting our breathing toward effortlessness. It felt magical.

We practiced *pranayama* for an hour, followed by a fresh vegetarian breakfast. After bathing and washing our clothes in cold water, we quickly rejoined our group in the central hall to meet the ashram *guruji*. With his calm face and Vedic wisdom, he introduced everyone to the principles of the code of conduct and a good demeanor for the betterment of one's life. Later, in an interactive session, he reintroduced us to meditation practices that help with living life effortlessly.

During our lunch break, we learned that the food they served—salads, fruits, and herbs, both cooked and raw—primarily came from the garden on the premises. Post-lunch, we were steered back to a centrally located open hall, and after a few questions, we realized we were attending a spiritual lecture. On that winter afternoon on the hillside, we were surrounded by trees; one could feel the breeze gently caressing our skin in that open hall. The lecture covered *Rajasic*, *Tamasic*, and *Sattvic* topics regarding food management that had been discussed in ancient Hindu scriptures. They emphasized how the intake of various types of food affects the underlying qualities of human behavior. I had learned those terms from my dad, a philosophy professor, but I was reintroduced to the concepts that day and became more familiar with them.

The lecturers explained the advantages of *Sattvic* food by point-ing out that we were all sitting there listening to an after-lunch lecture in that airy hall on the hill, and yet all forty individuals were wide awake, listening.

By four p.m., we were ready for the *shramadaan* session, when we would donate our services to the ashram by cutting fruits and vegetables or sweeping the floor. Some could also help out at the construction site within the ashram, lifting and laying bricks for the construction workers building the wall. The *shramadaan* was a very gratifying session; we were glad to be of any service to the ashram that so wonderfully enlightened us in this philosophy.

Our instructors had designed group games to teach us leadership and accountability principles. After the tiring games, we enjoyed a guided meditation session, so we might enter this joyful state of silence effortlessly before our dinner.

It was so refreshing and illuminating to find, in that structured program amid nature, that we never felt bored enough to crave our phones and lose ourselves in the mundane task of scrolling through social media. Later, sitting together for an hour with our group, we shared our insights from that day, surviving successfully without any technology or packaged food and, most importantly, eating only vegetarian food. It felt like a candid conversation around the campfire, except the only fire that arose was from our warm spirits.

The ashram curriculum made sure we ate healthy, raw, vegetarian meals, breathed clean, fresh air at that elevation amid the trees, stayed socially active by sharing experiences with our peers, and were mentally relaxed yet very receptive with the help of meditation techniques.

For the first time, I was experiencing life without my family in an ashram. Everyone seemed to be in a joyful state, and the whole ashram radiated happiness and bliss.

I realized I was living the best and most meaningful and yet meaningless days of my life, just being happy to be around, and for no particular reason. And those days went by swiftly. Three days were well spent on fresh vegetarian food and education on good demeanor, all while focusing on our journey to effortlessness.

Too soon, it seemed, the retreat was over, and it was time to return to our everyday lives. On the way back to Mumbai, the bus had an energized, festive atmosphere; everyone on the bus seemed friendly, cheerful, and optimistically energetic. Acquaintances had developed into a deeper bond of friendship; some strangers on the bus became my longtime friends. We began singing songs with the help of the bus's PA system. As a singer, I was always careful about my posture, but I surprised myself by effortlessly belting out a Celine Dion song on that bumpy, speedy highway ride. This was the best gift I was parting with from the past seventeen days' journey of *pranayama*. It was pure bliss.

Later, I pondered, *What was it? Why had this experience been so transformative for me?* All they did was explain the dos and don'ts that we had heard since childhood, then position us as leaders accepting accountability, yet they managed to tame everybody's ego and gave each of us a rationale on "Who am I?" They stripped us of our egos and tapped into the pure energy of each individual and attempted to polish the soul.

Overall, these seventeen days represented one of the best take-aways from my return to India, as these age-old yogic principles helped me reach that calm state required for effortless living in everything I do.

After returning home, we all continued our commitment by attending spiritual meetings held once a week in Mumbai, which helped us stay on that path and in positive energy. I feel this helped me maintain a calm state in life and prevented me from beating myself up over mundane demands. In short, I realized how much these techniques helped me overcome my challenges during my stay in Mumbai.

On the home front, we were all thrilled to see Mom slowly regain health and strength and resume her morning walk routine by now. I was glad to be around when she needed me, and I became her designated driver when she wanted to visit her cousins and aunt. However, during Mom's illness, what felt most punishing was being able to care for her only part-time rather than full-time. Besides, with all the commuting and coordination to reach Mom's place, it was especially stressful, given my other responsibilities as a mother and a business owner. This challenging time taught me a valuable lesson—no matter how far or close you are, you can't control the events around you or any other circumstances; you can only manage yourself.

I feel that the rediscovery of these life management skills that helped and guided me through my life has been one of the biggest blessings from our time in India. It almost feels like I made this intercontinental journey to receive this age-old, traditional yogic wisdom from my birth country. I am grateful for the discontent I felt for years in America before the move because that helped spur me on. Perhaps I was destined to return to my homeland and receive this precious wisdom of holistic health and well-being.

ॐ

37

This Wasn't My Grandfather's Mumbai!

It was eight o'clock on a Friday morning, and I was reading my newspaper while relaxing on the balcony chair. I was enjoying some me-time, as Neeraj had just driven Ronak to school before heading for his morning run.

Peering down at the balcony, I surveyed our plants, usually managed by our gardener. My balcony flaunted vibrant shades of orange and green with the flourishing *tulsi* and blooming marigolds during the monsoon months. I was engrossed in admiration when I suddenly heard the doorbell ring at short, intense intervals. I wasn't expecting anyone that morning, and as I glanced at my watch, I wondered who it could be this early in the day.

As I opened the door, I couldn't believe my eyes. I saw my maternal grandfather—Aajoba—smiling through the safety door, with his white stubble and neatly parted, white hair. He was dressed in his usual attire: a white cotton *khadi kurta*, white *khadi* trousers, and a gray *khadi* checkered vest, along with brown leather sandals and a sling bag over his shoulder.

I felt ecstatic—but I was also confused about the timing; I had not seen him in so many years. I touched his feet to show respect, welcomed him, and led him to the living room sofa.

"How are you, *beta*?" he asked.

"I'm so delighted to see you, Aajoba!" I gushed. "How are you?"

"I'm fine but perplexed; I was waiting for a rickshaw at Santacruz Station, and many rickshaws refused me the ride. I was particularly disheartened to see one rickshaw driver who took time to first spit on the road in my presence before answering me, no," Grandpa recounted sadly.

"Oh, Aajoba, I am sorry you had to see that."

He nodded, then continued. "So, finally, one old cab driver stopped without hesitation and dropped me off here without making excuses."

"Yes, unfortunately, things are not what they used to be in old Mumbai, Aajoba. The autorickshaws are abundant, but they do not want to pick up the passengers. They wait for passengers who are going farther."

He sighed. "Looking at some people completely turning a blind eye to their civic duties, I feel sad, and I feel like questioning them, 'Why?' This is not why my generation fought for our independence."

I agreed wholeheartedly. My grandfather dedicated many years of his life to India's fight for freedom from British rule. After completing school, he participated in the freedom fight movement until 1947. After India gained independence in 1947, my grandfather chose to remain a postman, turning down promotions in the General Post Office so that he could serve the general public. However, he also led postal employees by serving as their union leader. In fact, the older generation still remembers his name: "Dadhi Waale Rane" (Bearded Mr. Rane).

"Aajoba, I wanted to let you know that I am an American citizen now," I gently informed him. "When I was going for my citizenship ceremony in America, I kept thinking about you and the fight you put up for India's freedom. I know you fought for India's independence, and yet I chose to live in a foreign country. Hope you are okay with that." I wanted to get the weight off my chest as quickly as possible.

"It's okay, *beta*." He smiled. "You came back to your birth city. That's a tribute to my services. You are teaching Ronak his mother tongue, and he speaks Marathi so well. I am thrilled."

"Oh, I am feeling so light, Aajoba; all these years after gaining my American citizenship, I was so guilt-ridden whenever I thought of your sacrifices as a freedom fighter for India," I confided. "But you will be glad to know that, as it's now allowed in India, we have overseas citizenship of India and proudly call both India and America our countries."

I could see Aajoba felt relieved to hear this. "Remember, if you must do something, never do it half-heartedly. Own it." He continued, "Our generation knew that to get out from under two hundred years of British rule and to progress to the new era after India's independence, we had to own it all and honestly deliver that goal wholeheartedly, and that's how our generation helped the country."

"I wonder how you all did it back then," I mused. "It must have been difficult!"

He smiled. "We knew mediocrity was not an option; it was only achievable through discipline and hard work."

For the next five to ten minutes, my grandfather, with his hands folded on his chest and a glint of hope in his eyes, talked to me about how the country's future would be even brighter if everyone were mindful of their civic duties and responsibilities. He spoke so intently and passionately that his eyes turned red, just like when I had seen him in my childhood.

Once during summer vacation, my maternal grandparents had taken me to their native place in Konkan. That's when I had witnessed him deliver a very motivating speech in front of the whole village about the need to build a school there. His eyes had turned red when he talked about the disadvantages the rural areas faced in the absence of rudimentary developments; those fiery red eyes spewed his anger toward the social adversaries opposing building a school in that location. Even at the tender age of eight, I had understood the essence of civic duties, civic responsibilities, and the lifelong discipline in the life of a freedom fighter.

Relishing this chance to speak with Grandpa again, I offered him my take on the situation and explained that I had also seen it work better on the other side of the planet when people in America took responsibility for their actions. Then I turned the conversation to Ronak. "I always wonder if I did an injustice to my only son by bringing him to India, putting him on a different course of life."

"Why? Did he complain?" Aajoba looked concerned.

"No, in fact, he flourished. He adjusted to his new environment, showing great willpower and better conduct in a given situation than his classmates. I distinctly remember when he was in the sixth grade, the school celebrated August 15, Independence Day. They had their flag-hoisting ceremony followed by speeches. After that, the students were handed a bunch of hard candies with plastic wrappers. Most of the students ate the candies and dropped the wrappers on the ground. Ronak looked around for a trash can, but not finding one, he picked up the wrappers single-handedly and walked inside the building to throw them in the trash can. Other kids laughed at him and called him names. But he showed strong character and picked up all the wrappers. His teachers and the principal acknowledged his action as an excellent service to the school. Even in his final year, in the tenth grade, he challenged himself and delivered a speech in Hindi in front of the whole school," I said proudly. "Although English was the medium of instruction at school, he courageously chose to deliver the speech in Hindi. His classmates had teased him for his Hindi in his first two years, so he took the challenge and delivered it successfully. His determination, courage, and love for the language made me believe I must have done something right in bringing him to India. His principal also praised him on the dais for his Hindi speech. And Ronak earned the award of Master of the School. I was so pleased to hear that." My heart swelled with the pride only a mother could feel.

Aajoba shared my joy. He patted my back and praised me for teaching Ronak and inculcating the correct principles in my son.

We continued our chat till the doorbell rang again. I went to open the door, but the bell kept ringing. I was a little perplexed about why the door wouldn't open. I frowned, strained my eyes, and heard the doorbell again. As I opened my eyes, I realized I had dozed off while reading the newspaper in my chair on the balcony. Whew! So, I had been dreaming all this while? That explained how I could have seen my grandfather standing before me, clear as day, so many years after he passed away.

I rushed to open the door. As Neeraj came in, I told him about my dream, how baffled Grandpa was to see present-day Mumbai and the part where I got my grandfather's advice and his approval for being both an Indian and an American citizen.

I marveled at how all my questions about my grandfather's perspective had surfaced in my dream. It made me realize how much my loved ones' approval meant to me in those days.

ॐ

38

My Time-Capsule Image

I t took us five to six years to adjust to the contemporary Mumbai. When I reanalyzed my expectations for our move to Mumbai compared with my everyday reality, I gained a new and deeper insight into my own psyche and soul.

I slowly realized that the expectation to see that roaring monsoon action in Colorado's bright, dazzling snow was a longing of my own making. The Indian monsoon and the Colorado snow were equally impressive wonders of nature, but while I enjoyed the snow in Colorado, a tiny piece of my mind always thought it lacked the roaring action of the monsoon.

Similarly, when I yearned to see, and then felt ecstatic seeing, the wild bushes and the long, narrow blades of grass swaying in the steady rhythm of the monsoon breeze of Mumbai, it was a longing of my own making.

I had observed many extraordinary sights at tourist destinations around the world, but nothing truly compared to the monsoon's mighty roar and the vivid image of tall grasses dancing to the wind's rhythm.

The monsoon rain and the monsoon breeze always reminded me of my childhood memories that never failed to soothe my mind and settle my soul. So, when I returned to India, I unconsciously searched for the India of my childhood; that image had been preserved in my mind as if in a time capsule, where everything remained just as it had been: simpler, younger, and less complex. India remained in my mind in that form, and I never validated that image against the new India, which had changed over the past thirteen years.

As mentioned earlier, I had grown up in an environment where I was sheltered under my parents' loving wings long before I needed to make decisions for my child or my own household. Unsurprisingly, my worldview was somewhat limited during that period. So, in my "time-capsule" image of India, I assumed having maids and cooks to help run your household would be enough. But once I moved back to Mumbai, even though I'd been a pro at multitasking in America, performing the same tasks in a two-bedroom apartment with maids, cooks, and family around was still overwhelming. That made me realize that although I may have excelled at managing my professional team and work, I lacked the necessary skills to successfully manage maids and cooks in my Mumbai home.

In contemporary Mumbai, residents, for the sake of convenience, received multiple home deliveries every day. I realized that this was standard in any Mumbai home. While some households hired full-time help to answer the doorbell and phone calls, others who didn't have full-time help perhaps didn't mind answering the door. But our circumstances were different; Neeraj and I worked from home at night and needed quiet time during the day to catch up on sleep. So, we preferred help only for two to three hours of housework daily and chose to forgo full-time help. That's why it felt overwhelming, dancing to the tune of multiple doorbells and phone calls 24/7.

Before I got married, all I had to worry about was my job and a few chores around the house. Then, when I first arrived in the U.S., like most Americans, I took care of my job, cooked our meals, and split housework duties with my husband. Most people find that after running a household for a while, you become accustomed to doing things a certain way—"your" way. So, after we returned to India, we expected the maids to deliver the work to our expressed standards, and I was disappointed when I didn't see cleanliness and a recognizable level of diligence. However, I also realized that perhaps their grueling work schedules, which involved working at several houses each day, had an impact on the overall quality of their work.

As it happened so often during our years in Mumbai, I learned to adjust over time, still treasuring my beloved childhood memories while implementing practical, real-world solutions in a contemporary environment.

When I moved back to India, the changes I witnessed in the system initially seemed drastic to me. It shocked and saddened me to see the plight of my birth city, the herd mentality followed by some, the fast-paced lifestyle, and its unfortunate consequences—like some people tending to cut corners or take shortcuts to keep up with the increased pace. While it saddened me deeply to see these changes, I also understood that it was my interpretation of how I saw things. It was all on me for how I viewed the India of my childhood as contrasted with the India of today, just like I compared

India with the U.S. or compared Colorado's pristine winter snows with Mumbai's dramatic monsoon rains.

On a more specific level, I also became aware of the need to update and expand my expectations when I assumed I would find the same clean roads and comfortable public transportation in India that I'd been accustomed to seeing in America. But I'm aware that these comforts did not just happen overnight in America; it took more than two hundred years of democracy to realize those. In contrast, India is the world's largest democracy and relatively young at just over seventy years. I remain hopeful that my beloved birth country, with so much to offer, will continue to reach its highest potential as it matures.

Discovering these profound realizations about myself, my interpretations, and my expectations brings me back to the wise words of my dad: "Our ancient Vedic philosophy has always taught us about the impermanence of the material world. So, we must be ready to embrace change and move on instead of mulling over the past." I have found his words to be wise, and I have a new reverence for them now.

In the end, what mattered most to Neeraj, Ronak, and me were the skills we acquired and the way of life we adopted as we worked to unlearn what we had learned to survive on the other side of the world in America, and Neeraj and I also strived to relearn what we had forgotten—Indian ways. While I may not have ever rediscovered the exact India of my childhood, I learned to appreciate the beauty of the "new" India.

CR

39

Looking Back

I also had another important realization during those first five to six years in India.

I was invited to an art exhibition at the Jahangir Art Gallery in South Mumbai. Given Mumbai's road traffic, the local train system is considered the city's lifeline, so I decided to take the train and reduce my commute time. However, I hadn't traveled by train in many years and felt out of practice. When I looked at the overcrowded platforms, I worried I lacked the skills needed to board the jam-packed local train; that's why I reserved a first-class ticket.

When I boarded the compartment around midday, I was surprised to see all the seats occupied and a few women standing. I stood, leaning against the compartment wall away from the doorways, still clutching the overhead handle. As I got comfortable, I saw the adjacent second-class women's compartment separated by steel barrier rails. To my dismay, that train car was packed with people huddled together. Given the lack of space inside that compartment, a few women who were pushed halfway out of the train car door clutched the handles tightly yet showed no fear. I admired their courage. I noticed office-going women, college-age girls, and some schoolkids in that train car; in addition, three fishmongers tried to balance baskets of fish atop their heads despite the speed of the train.

Suddenly, I was distracted by sweat drops on my neck and forehead. Dabbing the sweat beads, I frowned at the ceiling fan in my compartment; it had stopped. I turned the switch on and off, but it seemed futile. I was annoyed with the humidity and the scorching heat outside.

But when I gazed again at that crammed second-class compartment, I saw women in *sarees* and some in *salwar kurtas*. Standing close to other women on that humid afternoon, they showed no discomfort at all as they balanced on the swiftly moving train. Almost every single one exerted patience, without a doubt. I was in awe!

Yet I was irritated; the scorching heat had me nearly attacking the fan switch, turning it on and off several times. Although dressed in the most comfortable summer cotton outfit, I was also riding in a relatively empty first-class compartment compared to that packed car. I couldn't even imagine how overheated those ladies felt, heavily clothed and standing so close inside that crowded space. But I had been away for thirteen years and had not witnessed this changing scenario. I was overwhelmed by it all, experiencing the heat without any fan over my head and merely glancing at the overloaded second-class car from my much roomier place in first class.

In the past, when I had worked in Mumbai, I was never so affected by the heat and crowd because I was accustomed to them. But, spoiled by commuting in an air-conditioned American car—which was a necessity in America, I had forgotten how it felt to be on an overstuffed train in Mumbai. That day, I also realized that all those women who seemed perfectly poised and didn't complain about the atmosphere, crowd, and circumstances had been part of that system forever, perhaps without missing a single day. The heat and bustling chaos I had been without for so long and was now fixated on had been their companion in everyday life and simply blurred into the background noise.

Today, I look back and think about our drastic and gigantic decision to move countries with our son. We sailed with no proper direction or definitive plan concerning our bread and butter. We dived into it without knowing how we would support ourselves, not sure about the opportunities available on the other side of the world.

But I now understand why we took this incredibly bold step at that time; I realize that it was a true leap of faith into the unknown. Not many people would change countries after thirteen years of a comfortable stay in one; we had no examples to guide us in this move.

In the end, I feel the three of us fought our share of battles to adjust to a changed India. It wasn't always smooth sailing for Ronak. He had his troubles fitting into a new educational system and a new society. Still, he conquered it all with unwavering determination. Because of his endurance, resilience, and willingness to go on, we were able to stay in India for nine years. Despite the challenges he faced and a steep learning curve, he made the most of the opportunities that came his way. It was gratifying to see him thrive. I take comfort in the knowledge that Ronak will fit in comfortably wherever he goes, in the same way he was well-adjusted in both countries.

For Neeraj and me, the India we had known growing up was

fading, and the kind of support system and household help we had assumed to be there was also missing. As my dad used to say, "No man ever steps in the same river twice, for it's not the same river, and he's not the same man." He probably got this quote from the ancient Philosopher Heraclitus, but having heard it from my dad helped me recall it when needed. We understood and resonated with this philosophy that everything is in flux and constantly changing, so Mumbai was neither the same city nor were we the same people.

I think, in my childhood, the people around me enriched my experiences of Mumbai. My father's cautionary advice, my mother's cooking and practical tips, my uncle's visits, my favorite aunt's phone calls, the giggles surrounding me, and the collective chatter of family members cannot be re-created to complete this experience.

But I am delighted that we planned our move and acted upon our decision instead of staying on the other side, left to always wonder, "What if?"

Having seen life from both sides, I now realize I can choose to be content wherever I decide to stay because both countries are near and dear to us. I feel blessed to be able to call both these countries my own.

CR

EPILOGUE

After the first seven to eight years of our stay in India, the time felt right to review my original hopes and dreams about this life-changing experience. The three of us were happy about our time in Mumbai, especially living closer to immediate and extended family.

Neeraj was glad that a work-from-home opportunity allowed him to spend more time with Ronak after he got home from school. When working from home was still a foreign concept in India, I loved that I also could work from home and invest my time in our company while tending to my family.

After I lost my dad, I was always tormented by fear—*what if Mom fell sick?* Most of us face these uncertainties, especially when we live far away from family, but I got worked up and helplessly worried about things I had no control over because it took me a long time to process my grief after Dad passed away. Being reachable in Mumbai, at least I was no longer preoccupied with these uncertainties.

After Mom's recovery from her illness, we were grateful to celebrate and host her seventy-fifth birthday party in 2017 with all her friends in a grand ceremony. With my sister's initiative, we proudly published Dad's book on the seventy-fifth anniversary of his birth, surrounded by renowned personalities from Marathi theater.

While living in Denver, we had visited India for four weeks every summer, using our entire accumulated yearly vacation time. Even so, this was never enough time for our families or for us, and we could never travel elsewhere in India on those summer visits. But once we had moved to Mumbai, we could take those family vacations to travel extensively to exotic locations both within and outside India.

We were pleasantly surprised by the wildlife wealth of India and loved our vacations in the nation's biodiverse jungles.

Survival Guide

One Sunday morning in 2017, I received a call from Nina, a friend from New York. After initial pleasantries, she said that even though we were reconnecting after seven years, I was the first person she thought of when she and her family decided to embark on the move back to India. It seemed she needed my help.

I stopped in my tracks. I was impressed and amazed at the same time. How could I guide her when I was challenged every day and still learning something new about this rapidly changing city? "My help? From India? Are you here?" I bombarded her with questions.

Nina said they were planning on living in India, and she was looking to me to guide her. As she described her plan, I could only tell her what I had heard from that wise lady I met in Rajasthan on our vacation in 2011, the woman who had also moved back from the U.S. Concurring with my initial challenges and disappointments, she had said, "It takes a solid five years to adjust in India, especially coming from America."

From my own experience, I added, "Everything is up to you, but it takes that long to unlearn our set ways and get used to this fast-paced life."

Hearing this, Nina said she was planning to stay in India for only two years.

Impulsively, I said, "So my advice to you is there is no survival guide."

But even as I said those words, I realized that I did have quite a bit of helpful guidance and advice for her. I told her:

- If you are in a metropolitan city, you are better off buying a car.

- If you are looking for a rental apartment, it's better to go with a newly constructed building with working elevators and regulated water hours. If you're buying an apartment, make sure you stay away from the major roads because the traffic is forever buzzing on the streets, even at two a.m. on weekends.

- Don't unlearn old ways if you are only here for two years; doing so will only make it harder on you when you return to the States.

- But do take advantage of the amazing biodiversity. These kinds of flora, fauna, wildlife safaris, and tiger safaris are not available outside India, so take as many excursions as you can in your time here.

- There is a treasure of Vedic wisdom on life skills and well-being available; try to learn it while you are here.

- The food here is the best. Try different kinds of delicacies from various states—foods that you won't get abroad.

I was happy to share with Nina what my family and I had learned on our journey, and I wished her the best of luck in her new endeavors.

I'm Here Now

Mumbai has always been welcoming, but the city is marked by its fast-paced, chaotic life, in which the crowd is an inseparable part of life. Yet this chaos also has an inherent rhythm, and if you move well or jell well with the rhythm of the city, you have conquered city life just like the millions of its residents. Once we jelled with it, it felt as if we had heard a song for the first time, painstakingly memorized its tune, mastered the correct notes, and sung it effortlessly.

I remember one afternoon, driving down M.G. Road with Ronak, I honked at a speeding biker who had overtaken my car. I had to step on the brake urgently; I lost patience and vented loudly. But controlling my anger quickly, I checked the rearview mirror. Ronak appeared unaffected by my monologue. Instead, he seemed relaxed as he gazed intently out the window. Curiously, I asked him what he admired on that busy main street. With a sparkle in his eyes, he said, "I love this market road. Everyone seems so engrossed in what they're doing. Yet this chaos seems well coordinated by every vehicle, human being, and the noise level present on the street. So, I love seeing it."

As I've said, it took roughly five to six years to get our grip on Mumbai's rhythmic yet chaotic pace and become fully habituated to the city. On the work front, however, after 2017, it was challenging to find an offshore project that allowed us to work from India. The demanding night working hours also took a toll on our health.

Around that time, Ronak got accepted into the University of California, and just like how our parents had always supported our education financially and emotionally, Neeraj and I chose to do the same for Ronak. I remember our parents' generation had come to Mumbai for bread and butter and stayed for their kids' education, leaving their folks in the villages. We had to do the same for work opportunities and to support our child, as a piece of our heart was moving to America.

My mom understood our decision and said, "You've got to do what's needed," and gave her blessing. We said goodbye to our parents, siblings, extended family, and Mumbai and came to California to get Ronak settled into his university dorm. Finally, we left him in his own capable hands and since most of our company's clientele was based in Houston, we decided to fly there and test the water.

Living back in the States now, I see well-planned roads, less noisy streets, disciplined traffic, and rule-followers around the streets; no bus tickets or cigarette butts on the road, and not a single biker driving down the wrong lane. Still, I sometimes catch myself missing Mumbai's chaotic rhythm. I am also re-habituating to American ways and unlearning Indian habits, as change is not easy for anyone but is also inevitable!

My current home city's spirit is quite different from Mumbai's. But after changing my city of residence three times now, I know it will take some time to get used to our new life and the unique style of the new city. We miss our parents, but we are glad that they are surrounded by family and extended family. Now, I remain hopeful that our new beginning in the Space City will carve out better lives for us.

ॐ

END NOTES

Chapter 2: The Good Life in Colorado

[1] *The Chronicles of Narnia: Prince Caspian.* United States: Walt Disney Studios Motion Pictures, 2008.

Chapter 6: Mixed Reactions to Our Move

[1] *Slumdog Millionaire.* United States: Fox Searchlight Pictures, 2008.

Chapter 32: Going to the Movies

[1] *The Adventures of Tintin.* United States: Paramount Pictures, 2011.

Chapter 35: High School Years in Juhu

[1] While this quote is most often attributed to Mark Twain, that source has been called into question by various sources.

❧

ACKNOWLEDGMENTS

They say that it takes a community to put a book together. My family has been at the heart of this community and was there to share the hopes and joy and bear the frustrations of the author.

This book is a testament to the unwavering support of my family. Thank you, Ronak, for persistently urging me to explore all genres, reminding me that no story is insignificant, and aptly understanding my thoughts while reading my rough drafts. My hardworking and ever-smiling husband always encouraged me and supported me through my difficult times and continues to do so now. For him, patiently hearing the countless revisions of the drafts was not tiring work; at least he made it look effortless.

I owe a huge debt of gratitude to my parents for instilling essential values in me, and especially to my dad, who inspired my passion for storytelling, and to God, who blessed me with patience, determination, and resilience.

Several friends—Aparna Natarajan, Lorenzo Martinez, Jaideep Adhvaryu, Kadambini Dharap, Thom W., and Sangeeta Jukar— were my beta readers, who read a few parts of the initial drafts—I very much appreciate their efforts and astute feedback. I treasure all of your friendships. Jaideep, thank you for reading the whole manuscript on priority. I cannot begin to thank Lorenzo Martinez enough for his encouragement and for assuring me that this is a good story.

Aparna and my cousin, Rajesh Sawant, helped as sensitivity readers, and I appreciate their contribution. As a fellow mom, I appreciate your insightful feedback, Aparna.

Advocate Vivek Anand, your helpful advice was invaluable.

I want to extend my sincere thanks to my publishing coaches. Geoffrey Berwind, your storytelling tips were priceless. Dr. Sarah Brown and Debby Englander, your insightful suggestions, guidance, and cheering at times were needed. Steve Harrison, thank you for your insights into the publishing journey.

I express my gratitude to my publishing team—my editors, Margarett Diehl, Elizabeth Ridley, Beth Lin, and Mozelle Jordan—who tirelessly helped me through various editing phases to perfect and shape this manuscript into its final form. I also appreciate Christian Adna for the front cover artwork, Rushi Tawade for the logo design, book cover designer Jerry Dorris, and book design expert Asya Blue for their essential roles in getting my book out into the world.

CR

ABOUT THE AUTHOR

Hemangi Sawant is an author, business owner, singer, and speaker.

As a seasoned information technology professional, she has worked for companies such as Compuware Corporation, Comcast, and Leprino Foods for over a decade and now owns a software firm with her husband.

Hemangi holds a bachelor's degree in psychology from Bombay University and a Diploma in Management.

Despite a successful career in IT, Hemangi made a conscious decision to devote her time and energy to writing. She has authored her debut memoir, ***Denver to Mumbai—A Story of Returning Home***, demonstrating her unwavering commitment to this journey.

A well-versed speaker with effective Master of Ceremonies skills, she has shouldered the responsibility of a national-level award presentation in India apart from being a Master of Ceremonies in America.

Hemangi lives in Houston, Texas, and when she is not working or writing, she relaxes, singing Bollywood songs.

Hemangi is available for speaking engagements.

For requests, please email her at Hemangi.writes@gmail.com or visit her at: www.hemangi.com